UNTIMELY MEDITATIONS

THE RADICAL FOOL OF CAPITALISM

ON JEREMY BENTHAM, THE PANOPTICON, AND THE AUTO-ICON

CHRISTIAN WELZBACHER

TRANSLATED BY ELISABETH LAUFFER

THE MIT PRESS
CAMBRIDGE, MASSACHUSETTS
LONDON, ENGLAND

© 2018 Massachusetts Institute of Technology

Originally published as *Der radikale Narr des Kapitals: Jeremy Bentham, das "Panoptikum" und die "Auto-Ikone"* by Matthes & Seitz Berlin: © Matthes & Seitz Berlin Verlagsgesellschaft mbH, Berlin 2011.

This book was set in PF DinText Pro by Toppan Best-set Premedia Limited. Printed and bound in the United States of America.

Library of Congress Cataloging-in-Publication Data

Names: Welzbacher, Christian, author.
Title: The radical fool of capitalism : on Jeremy Bentham, the Panopticon, and the Auto-icon / Christian Welzbacher ; translated by Elisabeth Lauffer.
Other titles: Radikale Narr des Kapitals. English
Description: Cambridge, MA : MIT Press, 2018. | Series: Untimely meditations ; 10 | Includes bibliographical references.
Identifiers: LCCN 2017047695 | ISBN 9780262535496 (pbk. : alk. paper)
Subjects: LCSH: Bentham, Jeremy, 1748–1832. | Bentham, Jeremy, 1748–1832. Panopticon. | Bentham, Jeremy, 1748–1832. Auto-icon.
Classification: LCC B1574.B34 W4513 2018 | DDC 192—dc23 LC record available at https://lccn.loc.gov/2017047695

10 9 8 7 6 5 4 3 2 1

For Vera, Kadidja
and for Elmar

I was, however, a great reformist; but never suspected that the people in power were against reform. I supposed they only wanted to know what was good in order to embrace it.

—Jeremy Bentham, conversation with John Bowring, London, February 2, 1827

I must praise my friend Bentham, that radical fool; he's aging well, and that despite being several weeks' my senior.

—Johann Wolfgang von Goethe, conversation with Johann Peter Eckermann, Weimar, March 17, 1830

CONTENTS

THE RADICAL FOOL OF CAPITALISM

Jeremy Bentham's Auto-Icon, produced 1832–1833. Today
on display at University College London.

THE THEORY BEHIND THE PRACTICE

Jeremy Bentham (1748–1832)—born within a few weeks of Johann Wolfgang von Goethe, the firstborn son of an influential London barrister, a trained jurist, a leading political and moral philosopher of the Enlightenment, and the founder of utilitarianism—was a theorist of action. With regard to the fulfillment of Being in happiness, he considered his deliberations not only useful but practical. He personally endorsed the applicability of his ideas, even beyond the end of his life. His final manuscript, entitled "Auto-Icon," discusses possible uses of the dead to benefit later generations. Bentham died before finishing the text, but the theories it contained were effectively sealed by means of his decision to have his body preserved and put on display. "He's aging well": to this day, "Bentham" sits in a cabinet constructed specifically for this purpose at University College London, armed with his cane and dressed in a frock coat and disproportionately large hat. As an Auto-Icon, he observes the goings-on and regularly receives students, disciples, and even critics.

An audience with "Bentham" immediately invokes a host of topics that defined his second seminal work of applied philosophy, the considerably more famous *Panopticon, or The Inspection-House*, published in 1791. First, what was the practical value of philosophical ideas? This question dogged Bentham all his life; it drew him out of the "splendid isolation" of the intellectual's existence and continually pushed him into conflict with the crown and Parliament.

Second, and connected to the first, is the question regarding the line between solemnity and jest. Bentham plumbed its depths with "radical folly," driving the question to conceptual and tangible extremes and into the realm of the absurd. Third is the question of the line between truth and illusion. In the Panopticon, this manifests in the impenetrable gaze of the warden, who monitors the cells with a sweeping view from a chamber at the center of the structure while remaining hidden from view, or "seeing without being seen."[1] As for the Auto-Icon, this question resides within the character of the effigy—representative images of rulers that circulated widely in eighteenth-century England and France, which were honored in place of the person and could even exercise jurisdiction in the Middle Ages. Fourth, and also connected, is the question of symbolic representation—whether of the body or architecture.

The questions Bentham poses feel familiar and current. Poised historically on the brink of the Enlightenment, American independence, and the French Revolution, the philosopher clearly knew to invoke *topoi* that would come to define the modern era and that reverberate to this day. In the Panopticon, Bentham saw a pedagogical instrument incorporating the tenets of reason, as it were. Construction and function, plan and influence, architecture and politics are brought into alignment. Bentham extoled the discovery in words that could easily be ascribed to Le Corbusier, Bruno Taut, or any other representative of classic modernism. "What is architecture?" Walter Gropius asked in April 1919, answering, "The crystalline expression of man's noblest

THE THEORY BEHIND THE PRACTICE

thoughts, his ardour, his humanity, his faith, his religion!"[2] In the *Panopticon*, Bentham writes:

> Morals reformed—health preserved—industry invigorated—instruction diffused—public burthens lightened—Economy seated, as it were, upon a rock—the Gordian knot of the Poor-Laws are not cut, but untied—all by a simple idea in Architecture![3]

Architecture (or the art of construction) as an agent of edification, or—in more general terms—culture as an agent of moral legitimation: this idea reflects a basic theme of sociopolitical change after 1750, which is closely tied to the emergence of the middle class as the dominating social stratum. This "bourgeois element," which pervades the anti-monarchic Bentham's works in various forms, cemented his reputation at the time as a reformer and "radical."[4] Bentham—who assumed that human happiness was not only quantifiable but tied directly to the pursuit of money and good(s)—was the philosopher of the bourgeois elite, the merchant class, and of capital itself. In a world after Adam Smith, he championed the view that economics' essentially self-regulating nature would recast society as a functioning whole, based on logic and a rational foundation evidenced in Creation itself. In response to this reasoning—and its resonance—Karl Marx unreservedly eviscerated Bentham.

In the 1960s, when the rediscovery of the *Panopticon* transformed Bentham into an oft-quoted object of philosophical attention, neo-Marxist critics sank their teeth into Bentham's bourgeois sensibilities and identified signs of reaction, if not repression, in his works. With his *machine panoptique*—a formulation that echoes Le Corbusier's axiom, "A house is a machine for living in"—Jacques-Alain Miller, for instance, implied the soullessness of moral-political intentions and administration's triumph over the emancipated individual of the Enlightenment, who inexorably becomes a prisoner of the systemic maelstrom.[5] Human as machine endowed with a soul and trapped in the cogs of a mechanized world order: this image would fit in the era of Henry Ford. But Bentham lived at the advent of the Industrial Age, which began in 1769 when James Watt patented the steam engine. The notion of human freedom always underlay Bentham's philosophy.

In Michel Foucault's *Discipline and Punish* (1975), the principles of panoptic surveillance and instruction—Bentham's "inspection principle"—are assigned an almost diabolical subtext that has its provenance less in the intellectual world of the English philosopher than in the projection backward of late capitalist phenomena onto the Enlightenment. From the perspective of the late twentieth century, the era of world wars and the Holocaust, the primacy of utility in Bentham's philosophy produces uneasiness. Many passages in the text sound almost prophetic—for instance, in valorizing human actions as carried out by the inmates of the Panopticon:

> Fifteen hours in the day employed in lucrative occupations: for in this regimen, be it never forgotten, even the time found for health is not lost to industry. [Note: Nor need the portion, if any, which may be thought fit to be

allowed to occupations of a literary nature, be all of it without an economical use. Such as could write well enough might copy for hire: at least they might copy the accounts and other papers relative to the management of the house. Even music were there a demand for it, might here and there find a copyist among so large a number.] Fifteen hours out of twenty-four without the smallest hardship, and that all the year round: not much less, as we have seen, than double the quantity thus employed in the establishments contrived at such an immense expense for the extraction of forced labour.[6]

Unlike Foucault, Bentham couldn't foresee the perverting of utilitarian thought, its being short-circuited by social Darwinism, racism, and their consequences. When Bentham proposed marking citizens with tattooed symbols[7] or envisaged the Auto-Icon, notions such as "extermination through labor" and lampshades of human skin were beyond the realm of the imaginable. When he defined "the greatest amount of good for the greatest number [of people]" as the raison d'état, the welfare state had not yet come into existence. And capitalism was still a pure economic system, not a way of life dictated by a global oligarchy of corporations after the end of political order. Bentham's starting point was the free subject, the autonomous individual seeking the path to maturity—not the consumer, a dehumanized object lodged between product and propaganda. And neither was education the "investment" it's taken to be today. The human soul had not yet been sent to hustle on the street corner of economics, on the hunt for "power" and "money," for one last shot at a game it had already lost—a game whose rules changed in the late eighteenth century.

There has been some speculation over whether the misconceptions regarding Bentham's teachings are based in the autonomy of the various lines of their reception. By 1820, when his publications on legal theory were made available in German, even his first works had long since been translated into French. From the early days of his career, and enabled by foreign language skills he lacked in German, Bentham had engaged in exchange with the intellectual elite of the Ancien Régime and the French Revolution, corresponding with Voltaire, d'Alembert, Mirabeau, and others. He found an enterprising "compiler" in the Geneva-based publicist Étienne Dumont, who brought his texts to the public, but not in their original form; instead, he published interpretive summaries. In the case of the *Panopticon*, which had appeared in France in 1791 as *Panoptique*, Dumont condensed the original manuscript's three disparate parts into a single text.[8] Rearranged, abridged, or extended passages and shifts in argumentation were the result. However authorized these versions, there is quite simply a French Bentham in addition to the English Bentham. Whether Foucault—as some critics claim—read the *Panopticon* in its *Panoptique* form (the complete translation of Bentham's original text did not appear in France until after the success of *Discipline and Punish*) is anyone's guess, especially since he didn't have a monopoly on misinterpretations and spoke English well.[9]

And yet: although Bentham research has been countering Foucault's theses with evidence-based analysis for decades, a clear view of the author of the *Panopticon* remains clouded to this day. Foucault's interpretations forced conceptual associations with the state apparatus in George Orwell's *1984*.[10] Jacques Lacan and his epigones went so far as to suggest that Bentham merged the concept of the sublime with state terror, expanding the spectrum of methods for "edification" from physical pain to psychological torture. These assumptions have shrouded Bentham with a sinister, bizarre aura that perpetually inspires new fascination—and yet they are based on a misunderstanding. Giambattista Piranesi's nightmarish series of prints, *Carceri* (1745), is as far a cry from Bentham as from Edmund Burke's concept of the sublime. Darkness in the Enlightenment—that facet so eminently important to its art and intellectual history—was only marginally reflected in Bentham. Instead, it was the bright illumination of the following insight that he viewed as crucial: that the individual's maturity and sound constitution, coupled with rationality and reason, form the core principles of an equitable order that finds its ideal expression in economics. In an effort to turn this ideal into an exemplary lived practice, Bentham devised the two great utilitarian projects that occupied him all his life: the Panopticon and the Auto-Icon.

THE PANOPTICON

PANOPTICON

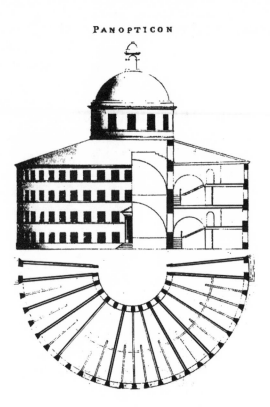

Design of the Panopticon. Ground plan and cross section by
Willey Reveley, drafted following Bentham's instructions,
1790–1791. Early version.

POTEMKIN'S TEMPORARY LABOR FORCE

The idea for a circular inspection house originated on a lengthy journey that took Jeremy Bentham to Eastern Europe. In August 1785, the philosopher departed London for Italy by way of France. From Genoa, he boarded a ship bound for Constantinople, traveling overland from there to White Russia. In February 1786, he arrived in the small royal city of Krychaw, approximately a hundred kilometers south of Smolensk (and not far from Chernobyl), where he was received by his youngest brother, Samuel. He would accompany Samuel for the following twenty-two months, until embarking on his return trip home, from December 1787 through February 1788.[1]

Samuel Bentham, a trained engineer, had emigrated to Russia in 1780 at age twenty-three and remained there for eleven years. He had found employment in the service of Prince Grigory Aleksandrovich Potemkin—the influential favorite of Catherine the Great, who served in her court as military general, minister, financial counsel, and grand marshal, supported by a personal staff stationed at his country estate in Krychaw.[2] When Jeremy arrived in White Russia, Potemkin was at the height of his career. Preparations for the Russo-Turkish War were underway, and as governor-general of the southern provinces, Potemkin oversaw the systematic development of huge territories. Samuel had found here what England evidently could not offer: a range of duties pursuant to his aplomb as an engineer and architect, which corresponded directly with the position of "artistic director" in an absolutist court.[3] Samuel benefited from the boom, and was elevated to squire at Potemkin's behest, maintaining his own manor in the village of Zadobrast, a few versts outside Krychaw. With a group of other planners, he led large-scale expansions of military and civil infrastructure for Potemkin. He built ships and called for the construction of canals and roads. At the same time, other architects were designing residences, farms, and villages that were so shoddily constructed that—on the occasion of Catherine the Great's inspection tour in the spring of 1787—Potemkin ordered provisional facades be built. To satisfy Potemkin's frantic demand, Samuel needed to manage hundreds of unskilled laborers; according to Jeremy, "a thousand men [were] under his command."[4] Permanent monitoring was needed in workshops built specifically for the task. In connection with this project, Samuel developed the first "Panopticon" in mid-1786. It was nothing more than an elevated platform, from which a single trained foreman or engineer could lead, monitor, correct, or "inspect" the mass of workers.

Optical centering was less an invention than the transfer of a spatial arrangement Samuel could easily have encountered in his academic training. In drawing classes for architects, engineers, or artists, objects are presented in a central, elevated spot and sketched by the students, who are positioned around the model.[5] The architectural manifestation of this constellation also has its roots in the academy, namely in the "anatomical theaters" first conceived in the sixteenth century. Initially little more than a wooden

Drawing lesson at the Royal Academy. From the series *The Microcosm of London*, 1808–1810, published by Rudolph Ackermann.

structure squeezed into whatever room was available—with risers that provided spectators an optimal view of the deeds taking place at the stage-like center—by the eighteenth century, the anatomical theater had developed into a distinct type of space, whose instrumentation and monumental stature served the glorification of the sciences. That Samuel's basic idea—itself no more than a simple transfer from Classical theater design—could provide functional flexibility for various construction projects is also evidenced in the Radcliffe Camera, a circular library building with a central reading room built in Oxford starting in 1737 (James Gibbs, architect).

Samuel altered the established basic concept to serve his purposes; he reversed the relationship between object and recipient, teacher and student, sender and receiver. He replaced the traditionally dominant, inward-facing axis of perception with its inverse, the point of view now originating

Anatomical theater at the University of Leiden, 1609.
Copper engraving by Willem van Swanenburg, based on a drawing by Jan Cornelisz van't Woud (Woudanus).

Radcliffe Camera, Oxford. Designed by James Gibbs, 1737–1749. Historic photographs of exterior and interior.

in the center and facing outward: the scrutiny of the overseer. Its optimization thus fell to the art of engineering. The laborers' workspaces were grouped by function and separated by wooden walls. Citing pedagogical considerations, he expanded the propped-up, revolving overseer's area at the center to a sort of pavilion that one could not see into from the outside, as Jeremy Bentham later recalled:

> It was considered accordingly, that it was material to good order, that the workmen, whose operations were designed to be thus watched, should not be able to know each of them respectively at any time, whether he was or was not at that moment in a state in which the eyes of the inspector were directed to his person in such manner as to take a view of it: accordingly, for the production of this effect, provision was made of an annular screen, pierced in such a manner with slits and holes, that by any person it might be seen whether a person, whom, in this or that other part of the building, he was taking a view of, was knowing whether he was viewed or not.[6]

The invention of the "inspection principle" described here reveals a remarkable parallel with its commissioner, Prince Potemkin: the notion of "as if." Samuel subjected his workers to supposed scrutiny in order to complete the Potemkin villages, themselves only supposed settlements. The game of truth and perception, or creating an illusion by technical means, further underscores the relationship between the Panopticon and the (anatomical) stage, which Jeremy

Bentham would later repeatedly invoke. Potemkin was the director of a visionary state theater that performed politics as the spectacle of the aristocracy. The concentration of the workforce is in response to this intellectual distraction in the upper classes, in that the centrifugal gaze is flipped to the centripetal. On the other end of the social spectrum, the same principle—simply inverted—serves in the surveillance of the lower classes. The double illusion thus reacts upon reality. It ultimately stabilizes the established system of social inequity, making it more effective.

With Potemkin's money, Samuel recruited twenty English master tradesmen—masons, carpenters, rope makers, metal fitters, builders. They were to oversee the laborers, a group comprising dismissed farmers and detained Polish Jews, Cossacks, and Germans.[7] The newly hired Englishmen, the "Newcastle mob" (Samuel Bentham), proved to be undisciplined and debauched. They even began to sabotage Samuel's construction of a panoptical dockyard. The plans finally collapsed in the summer of 1787, when Potemkin sold the Krychaw estate and relocated his activities and entire staff to the Kremlin.[8]

Jeremy, who had used his time on Samuel's estate in Zadobrast to compose studies for a comprehensive volume on the penal code, soon tabled the work he'd brought with him in order to work with his brother on refining the Panopticon's spatial composition. Together, they wove initial ideas into a structural whole, Jeremy supplementing the plans with a theoretical superstructure to use as a practical example for illustrating his thoughts on constitutional law. During this process, Samuel's concept gradually migrated over to Jeremy, where it was transformed: in the philosopher's mind, the disciplinary means intended by his engineer/ architect brother developed into the model of a universally applicable educational principle. Following contemporary literary conventions, Bentham penned a series of twenty-one letters, in which he outlined the concept in stages.[9] He confidently praised the "new principle of construction" as applicable to every type of building in which humans may require monitoring. The educational idea so important for Potemkin's laborers remained constitutive, regardless of whether the Panopticon be operated as a factory, workhouse, manufacturing facility, poorhouse, insane asylum, military or civilian hospital, school, or prison.

Back in England, Bentham began reviewing his letter collection for publication. He was disappointed to discover it represented a "first rough, imperfect sketch: imperfectly contrived and still more imperfectly expressed."[10] Did the manuscript come across as alien, now that distance had weakened his fleeting empathy for a "wrong" system incubated by proximity to power? Bentham had, after all, referred to Potemkin as the "Prince of Princes" with a mixture of irony and admiration.[11] He had tried to take seriously Catherine the Great's reputation as a reformer, and hoped to provide her legal counsel. He would have accepted the luster of autocratic association; what's more, despite his extreme reservations regarding aristocratic power and the doctrine of divine right, he seriously considered relocating to the Kremlin with his brother, to serve in Potemkin's new court as a squire and statesman. Were these the contradictions that preoccupied Bentham in rereading his letters? The Panopticon was clearly in need of a political foil to preclude awkward interpretations. This became all the more urgent as the fall of absolutism in France became imminent. These developments demanded clarification of the text's political implications, particularly as Bentham anticipated a wide readership on the other side of the Channel.[12] It was thus critical that the Panopticon by no means be viewed as an instrument for safeguarding established social inequities. Rather, it was to be seen as a relevant contribution to the sociomoral upheaval gripping Europe at the time.

At the same time as he was finishing work on the penal code—the preface to which was published as *An Introduction to the Principles of Morals and Legislation* in 1789, the year of the revolution—Bentham set about preparing the *Panopticon*. Rather than painstakingly revising the epistolary corpus, however, he appended two stand-alone annotated "postscripts." In twenty-four parts, the first ("Further Particulars and Alterations Relative to the PLAN OF CONSTRUCTION Originally Proposed") addresses structural problems in the architecture and interior spatial arrangement. The second postscript ("A Plan of Management for a Panopticon Penitentiary House," in sixteen parts) outlines the Panopticon's particular application as a prison, and challenges the social, economic, and political workings within state order as a whole. He aimed to show readers that the Panopticon represented the cornerstone of long-overdue state reform, whose implementation would secure England a position of political and economic leadership in Europe:

> Covered with the rust of antiquity, the law of mutual responsibility has stood for ages the object of admiration. Fresh from the hands of Alfred, or whoever else first gave it existence, what was the composition of this celebrated law? Nine grains of iniquity to one of justice. Ten heads of families, with walls, woods, and hills between them, each to answer for the transgressions of every other! How different the case under the domination of the inspection principle! Here shines justice in unclouded purity. Were the Saxon law to be reduced to the same standard, what would be the founder's task?—To give transparency to hills, woods and walls, and to condense the contents of a township into a space of 14 foot square.[13]

The three-part print version of the *Panopticon*, released in Dublin and London in 1791, was an imbalanced text. The two "postscripts" were four times the length of his concise letters from Russia. They were divergent in style, inconsistent, sporadically dashed off as fictitious Q&A sessions (with the reader's anticipated responses), and expanded by means of cross references and other details including sketchily presented examples, footnotes, exceptions, and their elucidation. In its new form as an example-oriented metatext of *An Introduction to the Principles of Morals and Legislation*, the *Panopticon* was a patchwork with an almost genius tendency toward the chaotic (as is the case, incidentally, with most of Bentham's other writings). Without an understanding of Bentham's views on morals and the state, and without having read *An Introduction to the Principles of Morals and Legislation*, though, the hypercomplex postscripts are nigh incomprehensible, and to this day, they are left out of nearly all new editions. If nothing else, the fragmented nature of the *Panopticon* is enough to foster the one-sided interpretations mentioned earlier.

Then there was another problem. Bentham knew that without a supplementary guide—a plan—for the reader, the plausibility of the accumulated text would remain incomprehensible, particularly as it centered around a physical structure. Upon his return, he therefore worked with the London-based architect Willey Reveley to develop Samuel's concept.[14] Bentham had met Reveley—a student of William Chambers and player in the Greek Revival movement—during a good three-week stopover he took at the English Embassy in Constantinople, on his way to Krychaw:

> As a remarkably ingenious man I have heard him highly celebrated by infinitely better judges than myself of ingenuity in that line. His character, which has something of singularity in it, strikes me upon recollection, as being as unfavorable to peculation as can well be imagined. Open, chatting, querulous, telling one man what another says of him, and much more apt to make quarrels with people than to collude with them.[15]

And now, that truculent Reveley—whose irascible outbursts had lost him building contracts on several occasions—was

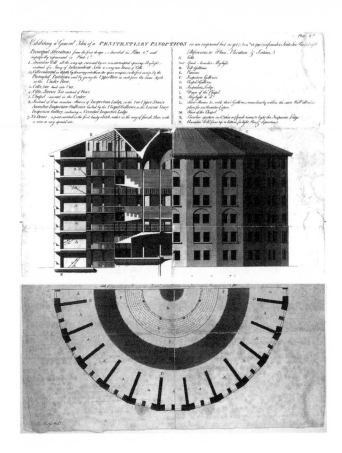

Design of the Panopticon. Unpublished illustration for the
1791 book.

translating Bentham's ideas into architectural drawings. He prepared floorplans, front views, and cross sections, along with three figures for the book, which (fittingly) reached the printer in Dublin late. Bentham's difficulties in coordinating the production process multiplied. In February 1791, he wrote in agitation, "A good part of my time has been consumed ... in acting as whipper in to Architects, Drawing-Engravers and Copper-Plate-Printers."[16] After the image templates had been reproduced, a fire destroyed the material; only a few pages could be salvaged. It was apparently too late for a reprint. Bentham insisted the text be published, and as a result, the book (but for three verified copies) went unillustrated. Later publications—an 1812 piece on caring for the poor, and an updated edition of the entire *Panopticon* in Bentham's *Collected Works* (1846)— were the first to present the text alongside Reveley's single, striking engraving, an annotated image depicting the layout of a standard floor, a cross section of the central structure, and the austere facade design.[17]

The lack of clarity in the first edition was even more troubling to Bentham as he awaited a response from the upper ranks of government. The work was addressed to Parliament, in the hope of sparking reform. Bearing this in mind, Bentham had emphasized using the Panopticon for penitentiaries and poorhouses. In so doing, he was responding to the politics of the day, the contentious "poor law," and the ongoing discussions surrounding penal law and its manifestations.[18] Additionally, a third postscript, bearing the title "The Panopticon versus New South Wales," criticized the practice of shipping criminals to Australia, lambasted the costs tied to senseless colonial control, and laid out a detailed calculation of the economic benefits the state would enjoy by housing its convicts in an inspection house.[19]

Before the 1791 publication of the *Panoptique* in Paris—which Dumont had condensed to a unified whole and put "in a French jacket," as Bentham said—the philosopher drafted a letter to the Assemblée nationale. In the France of the Revolution, which had begun with the storming of the Bastille two years prior, the linked themes of surveillance, education, and security had taken on new relevance. Bentham had seen it for himself, on a trip he had taken to a Paris shaken by political unrest in August 1789.[20] In the *terreur* that took hold a short time later, representatives of the Ancien Régime were detained in droves. From a utilitarian perspective, the scores of executions by guillotine were an economic waste. An inspection house, on the other hand, could put the prisoners of the old order to use in benefiting the new.[21]

THE HUMANE PRISON

It's impossible to understand Bentham's panoptic prison model without looking more closely at the English penal system and its practices in the mid-eighteenth century. Torture was an everyday practice. Some prisoners were kept like animals in chains. Others went unmonitored, corralled as a single group—regardless of offense, origins, gender, or sentence—in the dark subterranean dungeons of often provisionally repurposed buildings. The unhygienic conditions provided a breeding ground for sickness and pestilence. Death was everywhere. In their physically weakened state, many prisoners were unable to perform the labor imposed by their sentences. This resulted in renewed force and torture, and the cycle of suffering began anew. Furthermore, there were criminal acts between prisoners, murders and arson, and finally, uprisings that often spilled over (along with disease) into the cities and led to general unrest.

On behalf of the House of Commons in 1777, the aristocratic politician John Howard published a three-volume study entitled *The State of the Prisons in England and Wales*. The book caused a considerable stir. Howard recommended sweeping reforms to transform the underfinanced dungeons into correctional facilities.[22] Seeing prisoners as human beings meant investing in their well-being, providing sufficient nourishment and room to move, improving morale, and boosting work performance. Detention and abuse were to yield to education, with a goal unfamiliar at the time: rehabilitation. In 1778, shortly after Bentham's "A

BASTILE

A correct View of the Bastile, with its Ground Plan.

Repurposing medieval castles and forts as prisons: the Bastille in Paris. Historic engraving with ground plan, ca. 1790.

THE PANOPTICON

Fragment on Government" had been published, the thirty-year-old philosopher contributed his own essay on forced prison labor, as outlined in the so-called hard-labour bill.[23] From that point forward, Bentham viewed the major topic of the day—human rights—as closely bound to corrections, itself the unmediated outward expression of the political system. If the newfound self-assurance of the individual had propelled a fundamental renewal of political order in France and the United States, then English society could demonstrate its own humanity by bringing change to where it was least expected: among the poor, disenfranchised, and incarcerated.

Bentham's interest intensified as public discussions surrounding John Howard's report continued, culminating in the revision of English penal law and its tripartite implementation (1779, 1784, 1791). By the time Bentham developed the inspection house in 1787, the political-legal reorientation had already transformed architecture: with imprisonment introduced as the dominant form of punishment, prisons had to be established as distinct structures.[24] In addition to the cells, other functional spaces were needed: for instance, work areas and common rooms, gender-specific interior spaces and courtyards for recreation, a chapel, a fountain, and finally, separate rooms for the guards and a residence for the warden. Beyond these changes, Bentham envisioned clean prison kitchens, central heating, and ventilation, and even considered installing a spring water tank on the Panopticon roof to supply water directly to each individual cell.[25]

Giovanni Battista Piranesi, architectural fantasy from the
Carceri series, ca. 1750.

At that time, the new symbiosis between law and architecture could be experienced firsthand in London. Between 1770 and 1777, Newgate Prison—the city's main jail, a medieval institution at the heart of the city—was replaced by a new construction. During the so-called Gordon Riots of 1780, an uprising that engulfed the city in terror, Newgate was destroyed by fire and had to be rebuilt for a second time in 1785. In a visual display of penal reform, elements of aesthetic design were included for the first time. The mostly solid facade was composed of powerful, rustic ashlars; the plinth seemed impenetrably high; the eaves weighed heavily upon the walls; the Palladian windows had dead eyes. The unmistakable message conveyed by this *architecture parlante* was loudest in the decorative features marking the entrance. The tympanum above visitors' heads boasted oversized chains and handcuffs as architectural adornment.

Newgate provided the model for European prison design throughout the 1830s. Bentham criticized its style as expensive and gratuitous, because it missed the essential point. The prisoners inside did not benefit from being overpowered by the sublime; the overall complex and its functional structure alone could fulfill this purpose. Form as spectacle, form as décor: true atonement had no need for such ornamentation. The Panopticon's architectural form therefore wasn't conceived as a "speaking building"; instead, it was derived from and developed as a direct extension of penal reform. These premises were meant to be portrayed in the building's form and layout—the symbolism was not added on but intrinsic. The facade's clean lines and use of iron and brick (for economy and fire safety, as Bentham had proposed in the postscripts to the *Panopticon*) are reminiscent of industrial buildings, given the simplicity of construction and unplastered exterior. These solutions could be traced back to Bentham's architect, Willey Reveley. Architecturally, they presage nineteenth-century trends, such as the Prussian penitentiaries designed by Karl Friedrich Schinkel, and the Pentonville prison system, whose opening in 1842 would establish new design standards but whose draconian punishments fell far short of Bentham's ideas for reform.

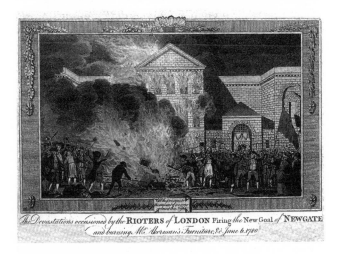

The Devastations occasioned by the **RIOTERS** of **LONDON** Firing the New Goal of **NEWGATE** and burning Mr. Akerman's Furniture, &c. June 6.1780

Fire at London's Newgate Prison during the 1790 Gordon Riots. Contemporary engraving.

Although Bentham participated actively in debates on the liberalization of penal law, his influence did not meet his own expectations. While the *Panopticon*'s missing diagrams may have hindered its broader reception, Bentham was tireless in advocating for its implementation. By 1790—that is, before the text had been printed—he was already seeking allies in a public tender for the project (hence his decision to print the book in Dublin). Alongside an advertising campaign aimed at finding suitable candidates to manage the inspection house, a model was to be constructed and Bentham's treatise circulated: fundraising to purchase a building plot. In addition to Reveley, the architect William Blackburn—the winner of a 1779 architecture competition for a prison designed according to penal reform—was also under consideration for the project.[26] In January 1791, a short time before the *Panoptique* reached the Assemblée nationale in Paris, Bentham sent his ideas on prison reform to English prime minister William Pitt. He was hoping for the prime minister to approve the project, which Bentham himself would manage, and for appropriate consideration in Parliament. In February, he negotiated with the Marquis of Lansdowne regarding a shipment of his collected writings, including the *Panopticon*, to the king of Poland. In May, he arranged for the book to be sent to the Society of Sciences in Haarlem. The *Panopticon* was—*pars pro toto* for Bentham's overall political philosophy—a global, universally applicable idea: "The different forms of the two governments present no obstacle to my thoughts. The general good is everywhere the true object of all political action,—of all law."[27]

Newgate Prison, London. Historic image of the edifice,
completed in 1785.

In May 1791, Bentham met brothers Robert and James Adams, the most important architects of their generation, who were then working on the Bridewell in Edinburgh, which joined poorhouse, prison, and reformatory in one. Robert Adam eagerly implemented Bentham's ideas:

> The Idea that struck me was, that by forming a plan entirely upon your principle, adapting it to our situation, our necessities, and within the reach of money we could afford to lay out; and by talking of this plan and the great ingenuity of the Inventor and the Invention, in which I always disclaim all merit, except insofar as relates to the above mentioned Articles, the curiosity of the Publick would be raised, the execution of a design upon Mr Bentham's principle insisted upon and that design to be carried into execution by me. / The alterations I have made may perhaps be honoured with your approbation, or at least may furnish hints for you to consider and improve.[28]

Adam cut the circle in half; the overseer's chamber, now a semicircle, protruded toward the cells, connected by a corridor (the backbone of the symmetrical facility) to administrative offices and two further semicircular Panopticons. The regimented layout was answered by artistic design. Adam, whose oeuvre is defined by monumental Classicism, borrowed stepped gables and turrets from medieval Scottish castles, which seemed plausible, given the Bridewell's origins in the palace of the same name, which was also used as a prison.[29] At the same time, the singular, historicizing

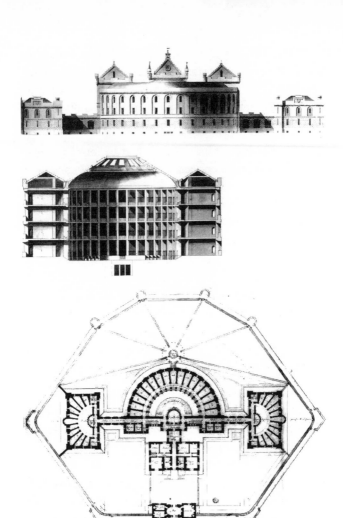

Edinburgh Bridewell. Design for a "penitention house" by
James and Robert Adam, based on Bentham's
descriptions. Exterior view, cross section, and ground plan.

THE PANOPTICON

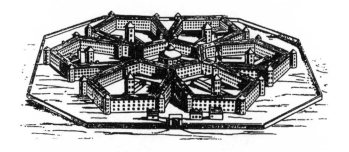

Millbank Prison, London. Planning image for 1712–1721 construction.

outline within Adam's work was a theoretical contribution to the design of prisons as a new structural type, which was evidently still assigned a mandatory—and medieval—style.

Despite isolated positive responses, the overall result of Bentham's international campaign was disappointing. The French, Polish, Dutch, and Irish Panopticons had foundered; England was the one remaining hope. In London in 1794, Bentham received parliamentary permission to construct a model according to his specs, what was to be the new National Penitentiary at Millbank.[30] He spent the next eighteen years planning the country's largest prison to date. Bentham clung to the implementation, writing dozens of letters, pamphlets, petitions, and diatribes. However, his growing reputation as a thinker, his contacts in politics, his occasional intentions to become a parliamentarian, his unyielding discussion style, and his antimonarchic sentiment invited ever new opposition to his plans. By the time

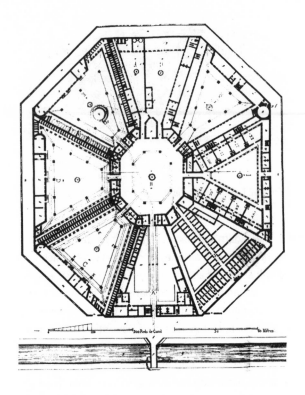

Maison de Force, Ghent. 1772–1775. Ground plan designed
by Malfaison and Kluchman.

ground was broken in 1812, these plans were diluted. The
ground plan revealed a number of wings arranged to form a
stylized blossom that only vaguely recalled the original idea
behind the Panopticon. By the time of its completion in
1821, the building had bested four architects (including

Robert Smirke, who designed the British Museum) and devoured the horrific sum of half a million pounds. Its creator, Bentham, who had been definitively shouldered out of proceedings in 1813, was tireless in criticizing "the Penitentiary" as a monstrosity and sought to blame King George III for its failure.[31] As compensation for his work, he contended successfully for a colossal fee of 23,000 pounds from his erstwhile employers, the City of London and County of Middlesex. However, he wouldn't live to see the realization of his allegedly "simple architectural idea," an alternative he would have preferred.

Whatever the fate of Bentham's concepts, there are many Panopticon-related aspects to be found in prisons built at the time. In his influential report, John Howard had already praised the Maison de Force built from 1772 to 1775 in Ghent. The full-fledged construction program of this "modern" prison represented a creative consummation. The wings containing cells and common areas flanked large courtyards and merged at an octagonal courtyard, so that the polygonal complex came together at its center. The desire for form and the work on the ground plan led Benjamin Henry Latrobe to a solution similar to Bentham's. In 1796, Latrobe—an associate of Thomas Jefferson, and the British-born architect behind the US Capitol—designed America's first state penitentiary in Richmond, Virginia, based on the country's liberal penal code.[32] The prison's large single yard was partially enclosed by a semicircular arrangement of cells. The entrance wing stood opposite, its central portal flanked by two guardrooms that opened

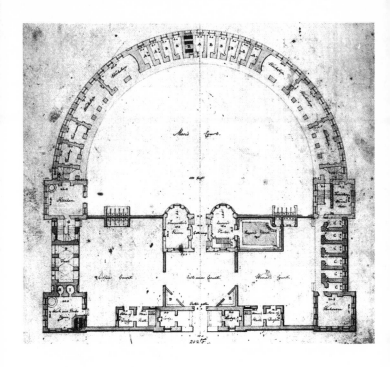

State penitentiary, Richmond, Virginia. 1796. Ground plan designed by Benjamin Latrobe.

apsidally toward the yard. The panoptical view from the window allowed surveillance of the entire open space.

Centralized vision as a leitmotif: this key aspect of the panoptical concept dominated prison construction in Europe and America from the last third of the eighteenth century onward. And although Bentham had little influence over

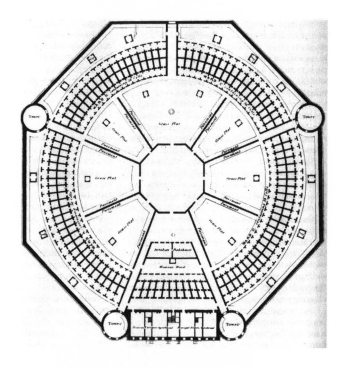

First Western Penitentiary, Pittsburgh, Pennsylvania. 1820.
The ground plan illustrates an increased centralization in
its design.

this development, the very comparison highlights how
exceptional the inspection house really was. Bentham condensed existing spatial concepts into a formal unit of
unusual coherence. He gathered up the ideas of the time—
moral, penal, social, scientific, architectural—and shaped
them into a symbolic figure whose political-philosophical

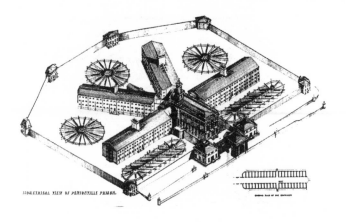

Pentonville Prison, London. Completed in 1844.

La petit Roquette prison, Paris. Completed ca. 1850
following Pentonville model. Photograph.

superstructure allows it to be seen as an emblem of social order as a whole. This totality, this layered complexity within something that is at the same time concise, is the root of the fascination with Bentham that exists to this day. It's what distinguishes the Panopticon from most other prison projects of the eighteenth and nineteenth centuries. And it's what shows that this is about so much more than a simple construction scheme: it's about a planned weltanschauung.

THE REIGN OF CENTRAL PERSPECTIVE

In his book *Discipline and Punish*, philosopher Michel Foucault linked the Panopticon to the Royal Saltworks at Arc-et-Senans, south of Besançon, built between 1775 and 1779. Claude-Nicolas Ledoux, the architect and director of regional saltworks in the province of Franche-Comté, had planned the entire facility anew, by order of King Louis XV. He was confronted with problems similar to those Samuel Bentham encountered in Krychaw a short time later: as his own business administrator and draftsman, supervising his workforce was imperative. He projected his organizational scheme onto the panoptical circular format used in town planning; in a second version, he modified it to be a semicircle. All of the public buildings, whose placement describes the circumference of a circle, are either associated with or subjugated by its center. The center of the ideal city is home to its administration; in Inspecteur des Salines Ledoux's case, his own seat towered over its smaller neighbors as a *"temple du surveillance"* (Ledoux) that enabled visual access to the entire compound.

While Ledoux's individual buildings in Chaux reflect the latest developments in Classicism, the town-like arrangement appears (intentionally) antiquated. The composition of lines, circles, and squares echoes the standard repertoire of absolutist city planning of the seventeenth century. In Versailles, known for its strict geometric structure, the palace stood at the center of the complex. The principles of central perspective, which had allowed for artistic control in visual representation since the Renaissance, are transposed into reality, where they facilitate idealized pictorial control over real spaces.[33] From the *corps de logis*—the intended nucleus of city and empire—the axes extend radially outward. The arts of city planning and governance are symbolically fused, in that irregular terrain is rounded off, land structured, and property parceled, developed, conferred, and colonized. In reverse, the axes head straight back to the center of power and vividly typify the divine right of kings, which couples worldly authority with transcendental sanction. In baroque planning, the axis is thus directly associated with the sovereign. He alone divides and distributes; he alone dominates and delegates. The design of cities mirrors that of the state. In many newly founded cities, like Saint Petersburg (1701) or Karlsruhe (1703), the admiralty (a nod to czarist sovereignty at sea) or palace was therefore placed at the center of the city plan.[34]

Ledoux adopted this politically symbolic schema in the saltworks as a stock expression, as if political order and the king's emblematic presence in the urban structure needed recementing. In Jean de La Bruyère's *Charactères*, his famous depiction of Louis XIV's court from 1688, the author states, "To call a king the 'father of his people' is not so much to praise him as it is to call him by his name or to define what he is."[35] Chaux's layout thus embodies the king's paternal proximity to the people, in that it projects a design paradigm borrowed from the royal court onto the "lowly" activities of a factory town, thus marking the saltworks as "kingly," or intrinsically bound to the sovereign.

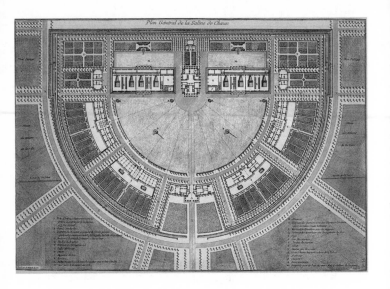

Chaux (Arc-de-Senans), home of the royal saltworks. Ideal plan for the city, second version featuring semicircle. Designed by Claude-Nicholas Ledoux, ca. 1777.

The "speaking power" inherent in this merging of axes and perspectives—in which political ideas transcend themselves to become artistic ideals (and are first perfected at that level)—is doubly underscored in Ledoux's composition. First, in the instrumentation of the administrative buildings, representative of the state: the martial effect of the surveillance temple is most obvious in the ashlar pattern borrowed from fortifications and used on the portico.[36] Second, Ledoux introduces a contrast (as far as urban planning is concerned): an antithetical area of bucolic ease just outside the

home of the overseer (*temple du surveillance*), designed by
Claude-Nicholas Ledoux, ca. 1780. Current view.

city, whose gently curving lanes and scattered buildings
reveal the influence of English landscape gardens. Staged
idylls of this sort, steeped in the banalities of superficial
response to Rousseau ("back to nature," "noble savages"),
were also created in Marie-Antoinette's Hameau (1783–
1786) at Versailles, the model-like miniaturization of a farm
where the queen could dress up and re-create "peasant"
life.[37] Ledoux thus conflates the extremes. "Idyll" and "control" vividly represent two sides of a coin that history has
termed "enlightened absolutism." The glaring implication
that the upper-class idyll was made possible only by a

robust public administration controlling its subjects corresponds almost exactly to the saltwork's political premises: the development of salt manufacturing and the king's monopoly were linked to an increased tax on salt that avowedly served to rehabilitate the ailing state coffers.[38]

By suggesting a relationship between Chaux's built politics, with its *temple du surveillance*, and Bentham's inspection house, formal similarities between city plan and building must be revealed, thus establishing analogies between the corridors found in city streets and indoor hallways. In fact, both plans are based on the ordering principle of an architecturally guided view and its triple function: it structures a space, creates a hierarchy of objects and subjects, and crafts the plan for an artistic, ideal image of actual power dynamics. While Ledoux's complex consists of three zones —monarchical divine right, controlled workforce, elite idyll—the sociopolitical relationship between the center and periphery of the Panopticon is more complicated. Bentham decided against designing an antithesis to the inspection house. None of the plans mentions "surroundings," since "free" humans were not being discussed. Nevertheless, Bentham did elsewhere develop ideas regarding ideal social conditions, which do offer an antithesis to the Panopticon:

> We shall never make this world the abode of perfect happiness: when we shall have accomplished all that can be done, this paradise will yet be, according to the Asiatic idea, only a garden; but this garden will be the most delightful abode, compared with the savage forest in which men have so long wandered.[39]

THE PANOPTICON

Karlsruhe. 1739 image of the royal residence, constructed in 1703.

Chaux (Arc-de-Senans). Ideal plan for the "periphery,"
designed by Claude-Nicholas Ledoux, ca. 1777.

The garden as an allegory of ideal social order not only
evokes Rousseau's construct of the human "state of nature"
but conjures religious parallels, as well. Bentham cites "Asi-
atic" ideas—Judeo-Christian mythology also envisions paradise as the untouched birthplace of humanity, an enclosed
but uncultivated haven of freedom (and not its theatrical
simulation, as in Chaux).[40] In this unadulterated, authentic
world, humankind does not (yet) require the normative
power provided by a planned space that represents it and
offers it a symbolic foothold. The architect, whose "simple
ideas" order the world, is superfluous. On the other hand,
the architect is indispensable in the place intended to edu-
cate humanity, to bring us one step closer to recovering the

THE PANOPTICON

Marie Antoinette's Hameau at Versailles. Designed by
Richard Mique, from 1783.

long-lost state of nature: the Panopticon. Design dominates here, condensed to functional form, legitimized by the nobler idea of a happier world—which can emerge only through the dissolution of traditional models of governance. In terms of Bentham's system, the two sides of the coin are *reform* and *education*.

In response to the French Revolution, Bentham had expanded his argumentation in the *Panopticon* by adding the two postscripts.[41] In so doing, though, he was undecided for a long time regarding whether direct democracy or constitutional monarchy presented the best option for new governmental beginnings. With regard to political systems, the

Panopticon was often in conflict with itself, in that it remained loosely formulated and open to interpretation, even after its revision. Bentham was, however, utterly assured in his criticism of conditions in France. English radicalism preferred the salon revolts—distinguished, self-deprecating, mutually cooperative. By the summer of 1792, as it became increasingly difficult to make reliable contacts who weren't sooner or later bound for the guillotine, Bentham distanced himself decisively: "Poor France turned into a Bedlam! Yet I am almost tempted to take a peep into one of the cells."[42] Bentham looked favorably on the fall of the omnipresent absolutism made manifest in Chaux, but he rejected the frenzy of the *terreur*, in order to clearly distinguish his ideas from those playing out in France and to position the Panopticon as a reform model couched in reason.

This observation has significant consequences for the comparison between Chaux and the Panopticon, because despite formal similarities, these projects are based on inherently opposed political ideas. Chaux perfects the nearly two-hundred-year-old model of a baroque palace complex as it reflects "enlightened absolutism," thus signaling the artistic climax and denouement of a development. Bentham's doctrine stands at the start of a sociopolitical departure that severs ties to the old order and declares its diametric opposite as its guiding principle: human rights. Bentham's penitentiary zeroed in on those people who had dropped out of society in the corporate state, imprisoned as useless objects. The humanitarian shift in perspective made it possible to see prisoners as individuals, to provide them

"The Contrast": an allegorical caricature of life in
revolutionary France versus that in restorative England.
John Rowlandson, 1791–1792.

support in their return to society, and—conversely—to
thus make them useful to the state again. Worlds separate
Chaux from Bentham's Panopticon. Foucault's decontextu-
alized comparison of the surveillance motif is fundamentally
misleading.

ECONOMY AS MORALITY

We must not overlook the incomparable nature of the political systems in France and those in Bentham's home country. A hundred years before the French Revolution, the
Glorious Revolution of 1688 had seen to the introduction of
a parliamentary monarchy.[43] Legislation, taxation, and judicial authority passed from the king to the (royally appointed)
Parliament and its two chambers, which reflected the political will of the various classes (crown, peerage, commonal-
ity) by means of two parties, the conservative Tories and
progressive Whigs. Suffrage was reserved for "free men"—
that is, those who owned property or belonged to a guild—
and of the 7.5 million people living in mid-eighteenth-century
England, these were requirements that a mere 245,000 men
could fulfill.[44] The country was effectively an economic
oligarchy.

The sensitive system of reciprocal political loyalty found
its symbolic form in Bath, the absolute antithesis of Chaux.
From 1724 onward, the yearly summer relocation of the
court—and with it, political life—to this prosperous spa
town in southern England led to the town's development.[45]
The planning reflects the upper class's basic understanding
of state, in that individuality is abolished and representation
appears collectively leveled. The residences for the aristocracy and bourgeoisie (each distinct in layout and size) that
comprise the summer palace are drawn together in a
terrace—a block of row houses with a joint facade—the
exterior embellished with palatial details. The proportion of

each individual unit corresponds to the whole, and to remove a single part would destroy the overall order. The city plan does not center attention on the king, nor is there a prominently situated royal residence. The presence of the monarchy is evident in place names alone (Queen Square, Royal Crescent). By absolutist standards, Bath can scarcely be considered a royal capital. In the English sense, however, it represents the ideal image of a class-specific division of power within a tiered elite that runs the state out of a shared interest and with mutual consideration.

The Royal Crescent, Bath. Designed by John Wood, the Younger, from 1750. Aerial image.

By the time construction in Bath concluded, the ideal-ized equilibrium in power (the "law of mutual responsibility" received "fresh from the hands of Alfred," as Bentham had sardonically written) had long since eroded. Nepotism and alliances to secure personal interests had become com-monplace. George III, crowned in 1760, launched an offen-sive to renovate Parliament by manipulating members loyal to the king. Although the intrigue fueled discontent among the people, the world's first naval and trading power contin-ued to profit from the economic boom of colonial rule in India, China, America, and Australia. Even the secession of the thirteen American colonies on July 4, 1776, and the ensuing Revolutionary War which lasted until 1783, could be compensated economically. From an intellectual, political, and moralistic perspective, however, these events had con-siderable consequences. The United States had taken deci-sive action to abandon the English model, placing new focus on voting and human rights, representative democracy, and the "separation of powers" proposed by Charles-Louis Montesquieu in 1748, which provided that the three govern-mental branches operate independently, while mutually scrutinizing the others' actions, in order to obviate systemic encrustation.[46] With this concrete example playing out in real time, internal political pressure was growing in London. "Reform" became the battle cry of the time. It applied to the prison system, taxes, foreign policy, religious practice, and ultimately the entire political order and citizens' rights. An alliance of reformers who went by the nom de guerre "radi-cals"—a group that would soon include Bentham—invoked both Montesquieu and Jean-Jacques Rousseau's notion

THE PANOPTICON

of humans' "natural rights," from which they derived the concept of "popular sovereignty." The result was a demand for voting rights without class or income restrictions.

Over the course of the 1770s, the exchange between reformers and government took on a sharper tone, and public scandals became more frequent. The courage displayed by William Beckford during this time became the stuff of legend; in May 1770, Alderman Beckford—a merchant who had made his fortune in the colonies and twice served as Lord Mayor of London, in 1762 and 1769—publicly challenged King George III to replace the members of Parliament loyal to the king.[47] The king was so enraged by the breach of protocol and violation of etiquette that Beckford ascended to hero status among the radicals. When he died a short time later, the London Common Councilmen—stronghold of the bourgeoisie, merchant class, and antimonarchists—erected a memorial in Guildhall, London, the first statue of its kind in the Gothic town hall. Beckford's speech against King George III is printed in gold letters at the base of the monument.[48] Ten years later, the monarchy's response to these tensions was no longer so lenient or sublimated. In 1780, discussions about overdue reform to policies regulating religious freedom led to pogrom-like riots against Catholics. The Gordon Riots in London lasted for five days. The mob chased parliamentarians and members of the bourgeoisie out of the city, and before the uprising could be quashed, the rioters set fire to the newly constructed Newgate Prison.

British philosophy developed an alternative to the corruptibility of political power by invoking the lawfulness of economics. In his 1776 book, *Wealth of Nations*, Adam Smith

Design for the first statue of William Beckford, mayor of London. John Francis Moore, 1768. This antecedent of the statue in Guildhall today stands in Ironmongers' Hall, London.

THE PANOPTICON

had conflated aspects of Thomas Hobbes's and John Locke's political theories, yielding an unprecedented central idea; in the nineteenth century, heavily influenced by Bentham's protégé John Stuart Mill, this idea would be condensed to "economic liberalism," influencing twentieth-century capitalism and shaping ideological debates to this day:[49] the idea of a self-regulating economy as a system that hinges on human interests. Bentham followed Smith's argumentation in that he viewed the market as a moral system whose intrinsic logic promoted a yearning for goods and goodness, which in this way stabilized society. The subsidy economy (mercantilism) should therefore be abandoned, the ties between (already eroded) politics and economy dismantled, and the state restructured under the primacy of economics. These demands marked the transformation of what had been the economically informed self-assurance of the bourgeoisie into an immensely potent vision for society.

While Bentham expanded the economic models of the Enlightenment, he rejected new legal theories of the day. He railed against the "natural rights" of humans championed by other radicals, dismissing Rousseau's neologism as a "perversion of language" and "nonsense upon stilts." Rights and law weren't naturally occurring; instead, they were matters of sovereign force. They were conceived and managed by humans. The sovereign was there to ensure this was done in proper fashion. The regulatory power of rationality alone provides the foundation for the "greatest happiness of the greatest number (of people)." The freer the human as an economic individual, the closer he or she would come to happiness—or, in economic terms, profit. Bentham's ideal state is therefore a society of happy work, which cannot be attained without education.[50] To create a model that illustrated humans' relative strengths, but also in order to discipline them in reality, and within the parameters of this ethos, the philosopher developed the Panopticon.

Bentham's pedagogical ambitions did not pertain to the inmates alone; rather, they even included prison administration. The microcosm of the prison provided fertile ground for the powers of the free market to start effecting societal reform. The pursuit of maximum economic success—which Bentham equated with the pursuit of happiness—stood in direct natural opposition to any abuse of power or repression of prisoners. Ideally, economics and morality exist in a symbiosis yielding shared benefit, since good treatment of prisoners accelerates the desired educational success; prison labor is performed more conscientiously; and—in short—the humane behavior of prison administration inevitably leads to an increase in profit. The call for prison privatization—a discussion making headlines again today—is Bentham's doing.[51] Only when the Panopticon is run like a corporation, free from political regulation, can the system effectively regulate itself and bring about goodness and happiness for all parties involved. Based on Adam Smith's teachings, Bentham thus designed an autonomous microcosm that can stand, *pars pro toto*, for a future ideal state built on the foundation of economic liberalism.

> Economy ... should be the ruling object. But in economy everything depends upon the hands and upon the terms.

In what hands then?—Upon what terms? These are the two grand points to be adjusted: and that before any thing is said about regulations.—Why?—Because as far as economy is concerned, upon those points depends, as we shall see, the demand for regulations. Adopt the contract-plan, regulations in this view are a nuisance: be there ever so few of them, there will be too many. Reject it, be there ever so many of them, they will be too few. / Contract-management, or trust-management? If trust-management, management by an individual or by a Board? Under these divisions every possible distinct species of management may be included. You can have nothing different from them unless mixing them. ... / By whom then, shall I say, ought a business like this to be carried on?—By one who has an interest in the success of it, or by one who has none?—By one who has a greater interest in it, or by one who has an interest not so great?—By one who rakes loss as well as profit, or by one who takes profit without loss? By one who has no profit but in proportion as he manages well, or by one who, let him manage ever so well or ever so ill, shall have the same emolument secured to him? These seem to be the proper questions for our guides. Where shall we find the answers?—In the questions themselves and in the Act.[52]

The universal key to appropriateness in corrections lies in the concept of efficiency. In terms of success and humanity—impelled by his instinctive pursuit of profit—the overseer will complete the prisoners' education as quickly as possible, delivering the delinquents into new working conditions outside the institution: "The end in view here is to ensure the good behaviour and subsistence of convicts after the expiration of their punishment, regard being had to economy, humanity, and justice."[53] The inmates of the Panopticon are thus everything they weren't allowed to be down in the dungeons: part of society, human beings, economic subjects who had the right to happiness and a life after their time in the inspection house. In order to comprehend this, management needs "soft skills," including appropriate communication. This is determined by the purpose and location of each Panopticon and involves various leadership skills.

> For the Poor-house of a single Parish what can you expect better than some uneducated rustic or petty tradesman? the tendency of whose former calling is more likely to have been of a nature to smother than to cherish whatever seeds of humanity may have been sown by nature. For a station as so conspicuous and public a kind as that of the Governor of a National Penitentiary-House, even upon the footing of a contract, men of some sort of liberality of education can scarce be wanting: men in whose bosoms those precious seeds have not been without culture. Such men were certainly not wanting for the originally designed Penitentiary-House. Upon what principle should they ever be despaired of for what I hope I may stile the improved one? In a concern of such a magnitude, the profit if it be any thing can hardly be inconsiderable: the number and quality of the candidates may be expected

to be proportionable. A station that is at any rate con-
spicuous, and that may be lucrative, a station in which
such good as well as much evil may be done, in which
no inconsiderable merit as well as demerit may be displayed in a line of public service, is in little danger of
going a begging. And should the establishment be for-
tunate in its first choice, the reputation of the servant
will help to raise the reputation of the service.[54]

THE POLITICS OF SYMBOLIC FORM

Bentham as the godfather of "pure" capitalism: this school of thought appears hasty in its conclusions, as it embraces a fractured sense of the philosopher's overall system of thought.[55] In addition to politics and economics—and one hundred years before Nietzsche, no less—Bentham naturally considered the third major organizational system in his configurations of the inspection principle, namely religion. In the first postscript to the Krychaw letters, a few pages after his remarks on the market economy, Bentham introduces the representation of a godly order to the Panopticon. The 1787 planning did not include a chapel. In the 1791 revision, however, the chapel became the structure's central feature: it came to occupy the eye of the Panopticon, illuminated by the heavenly light spilling through the oculus in the dome, itself a motif quoting the Roman Pantheon, a circular temple honoring the gods, and used widely in Christian institutional architecture.[56]

The pathos of this symbolic instrumentation presents metaphysics as the central moral authority. Bentham highlights this further in his representation of economics in the layout of the Panopticon, which appears to be an afterthought. Meeting rooms and administrative offices appear inconsequential in juxtaposition with the mighty axes of power between Heaven and Earth, center and periphery. Reviewing Bentham's political theory, the conclusion emerges: the systemic order of economic liberalism moves the individual into direct proximity to God, a position

unattainable for large swaths of the population under absolutism. This new freedom, the freedom of the bourgeoisie,
opens the autonomous path to happiness on the basis of
economic legitimacy, governed by overarching religious and
moral guiding principles.

From an entirely practical perspective, the functional
expansion of the Panopticon led to difficulties in planning.
Until that point, the building had been little more than a roof
over Samuel Bentham's "invention" in Krychaw—a central

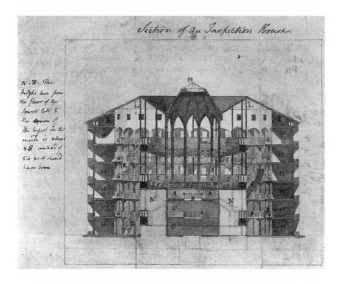

Cross section of the Panopticon with expanded room
system, ca. 1791. Drawing by Willey Reveley following
Bentham's instructions. The domed chapel is located at the
center of the upper floors, with the warden's chambers
below.

inspection pavilion encircled by cells. In the updated construction, however, the chapel and overseer's inspection chamber were now in competition for the center of the structure. Bentham's architect Willey Reveley did not solve the problem (like Robert Adam in Edinburgh) through variation (halving) of form and integration in a larger complex—instead, he used a trick.[57] In the floorplan, both features appear in the same location—the cross section alone reveals that the chapel occupies the upper stories of the Panopticon, while the inspection room is relegated to the levels below. Stacking these central features helped maintain the relationship between the center and ring of cells, and thus the desired symbolic formulation of the inspection principle. In practice, however, the panoptical view would have been substantially compromised.

The introduction of an ideal authority provided the inspection house with an argumentative backbone far beyond the economic instrumental rationality that had been postulated. Faith and religion made the radical, innovative theories more palatable, in that they fell back on comfortable platitudes and conciliatory tradition. Bentham also had recourse to the *topos* of the battle between godly and worldly deliverance, a major aspect in John Bunyan's influential 1687 allegory, *The Pilgrim's Progress*. On his pilgrimage to deliverance, Bunyan's protagonist, Christian, encounters Mr. Worldly Wiseman, who directs him to visit the village of Morality, where Mr. Legality and his son Civility will guide him in seeking salvation through the Law. But the path to the village proves impassable.[58] The

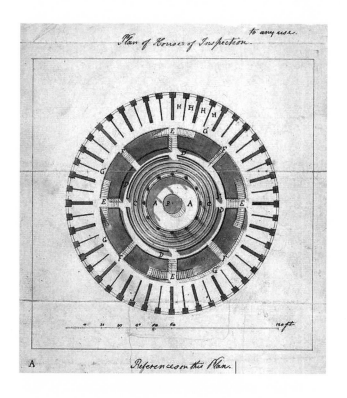

Ground plan with expanded room system, ca. 1791.

protagonist experiences representative failures when facing the hindrances that degrade the effectiveness of human systems. He changes the route of his journey, searching instead for God, and achieves deliverance. It would seem as though Bentham hoped to provide the inmates of the inspection house with this very opportunity. This simplified, traditionally moralistic reading of the Panopticon, framing it as a kind of secular church, is thus possible. Bentham illustrated the point in his discussion of Sunday Bible lessons:

> Of what nature shall the employment be at those times?—Let religion pronounce, the answer cannot be long to seek. Two modes of occupation present themselves: exercises and devotion; and lessons of instruction in such acquirements as are capable of being inlisted in the service of devotion. That the whole extent of the time could not be exclusively appropriated to the former purpose, is obvious enough: the very sentiment is more than will be to be found, until it be planted by instruction, in such corrupt and vacant minds. Paternosters in incessant repetition, with beads to number them, may fill up, if you insist upon it, the whole measure of the day: but the words, instead of being signs of pious thoughts, would be but so many empty sounds, and the beads without the words would be of equal efficacy.[59]

Despite an entrenched skepticism regarding the fruits of religious practice, Bentham adapted a centuries-old, fundamental principle of lived faith. The mixture of practice and devotion, spiritual exercise and surrender, prayer and work was intended to prompt inmates of the inspection house to introspection. This process involved the rational consideration of one's own situation as much as it did the emotional aspect. The law may dictate the measure of atonement commensurate with guilt, but moral recognition of the ruling's validity must develop within the delinquents themselves. Sin is expurgated not by the law but by the heart, through contrition and penitence. The strict regimentation of monastic life thus provided a starting point for the organization of the Panopticon beyond the separation of genders and housing in "cells," which had become common practice through prison reform. Bentham transferred the term "penitention" directly to the Panopticon: his failed long-term Millbank project bore the programmatic title "the Penitentiary," which would later become a general term for prisons. In this way, the establishment of societal stability and economic efficiency in the Panopticon is always linked to morality, whose religious origins function in their purest form in the laws of economics (and not, Bentham argued, in the "corrupt" church).

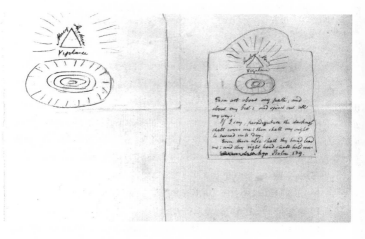

Bentham's design for a frontispiece of the *Panopticon*.

Superimposed image of ground plan, "eye of God," and motto of "Mercy, Justice, VIGILANCE." Drawing by Willey Reveley, 1791.

Beyond this, Bentham underscored the requisite quantum of sanctity in the design of a frontispiece meant to open the first edition of the *Panopticon*. It shows an "eye of God," circumscribed by the terms "Mercy," "Justice," and "VIGILANCE," arranged around a triangle. The words "Mercy" and "Justice" flank the sides of the triangle; "Vigilance," in particular, written in capital letters under the triangle's base, is highlighted as the fundamental aspect of the inspection principle. Additionally, an excerpt from Psalm 139 is printed beneath the drawing; Bentham rearranged the verses in order to exaggerate salient themes contained within the original for his own purposes.[60] God is invoked as a guardian and leader, as a companion to wayward souls, who—despite a familiarity with temptation—yearn for a return to the bosom of order and morality.

Bentham thus ascribes a religious motto to the entire Panopticon project, the radiant aureole of the "eye of God," a prevalent symbol of godly wisdom and justice since the seventeenth century, casting its light on the whole. Given the text girding the symbol's triangular frame—itself originally an abbreviation of the Holy Trinity[61]—its meaning appears to expand from religion to politics. The trinity of the inspection principle, seconded by that of the separation of powers, parallels the three manifestations of God. In a further analogue with the trinity, the manifestations of state structural powers also complement one another, joining in a superordinate whole. An illustration by Reveley, based on Bentham's 1791 frontispiece, demonstrates just how convinced the philosopher was of the Panopticon's symbolic simulation of societal power dynamics. The image shows the beaming eye of God (enclosed by triangle and text), projected onto the center of the Panopticon floorplan. The logo, in which the eye of God occupies the position of the panoptical overseer, fuses Bentham's intentions in a striking visual metaphor: the Panopticon becomes emblematic of the idea of the state.

Not many philosophers gave in to the allure of dressing their concepts in visually powerful ciphers. With figurative brevity always comes the danger of oversimplification. Bentham tested various forms of communication by complementing the primary medium of language with visual strategies, combining the "factual" medium of an architectural design with emotionally potent symbols. In the ambitious endeavor to contain the new conception of state order in an image, however, Bentham could invoke an influential predecessor: Thomas Hobbes, one of the few thinkers who had expressed his political theory by means of allegory, in his case the homunculus *Leviathan*.[62]

In the state, Hobbes envisaged an institution of security in which the willpower inherent in intellect would vanquish the ungovernable impulses of the human state of nature to overcome the chaos of freedom, the battle of each individual versus his or her neighbors. Hobbesian laws have a certain straitjacket quality. *Leviathan* was written in 1650, at the time of the English Civil War, an age of destruction and decay. Bentham's *Panopticon* appeared in 1790, in the age of revolutionary awakening. The two models' concepts of humanity and the state are contradictory: from the end of the seventeenth century, utilitarianism had emerged in the works of such philosophers as Lord Shaftesbury, David Hume, Adam Smith, and Francis Hutcheson, whose views were couched in criticism of Hobbes's notion that egoism was the basic instinct determining human behavior. The utilitarians ascribed to humans a degree of social instinct and the capacity for reason, qualities that would prove indispensable in fulfilling the primal human need for happiness. With his striking depiction of utilitarian tenets, Bentham was reacting to Hobbes's *Leviathan*: the frontispiece of the *Inspection Principle* was intended as a response to that of the homunculus, the image opening every Hobbes publication into the eighteenth century.

Critical to defining the cipher's scope of significance is the fact that Bentham was adopting a tried-and-tested symbolic language of the time. The eye of God, introduced to iconography by way of religious mysticism, also made an early appearance in the secular world, as a medal conceived in 1660 in honor of King Charles II.[63] The icon bundled those metaphors reserved for a monarch, such as the sun, wisdom, or equality with God; for that very reason, it also served in the struggle for freedom as an object of postmonarchical appropriation, becoming an image of a just order and sovereignty of the people. In 1776, Thomas Jefferson and Genevan artist Pierre Eugene du Simitiere proposed a design of the Great Seal of the United States that included the eye of God alongside the motto *E pluribus unum* ("Out of Many, One"). Flanked by allegorical figures, the eye of God also hovers above the written declaration of human and civil rights, drawn up with the king's approval in August 1789, by the French Assemblée nationale. The shift in context was thus consummated. The eye of God had become the expression of human autonomy on the path to God, the emancipation of the (bourgeois) individual through overcoming the old system: to wit, the ur-symbol of political rebirth. Despite his critical stance on developments in France and America, Bentham adopted the icon because it was recognized as a sign of political reform in the context of the Enlightenment and democracy; it could therefore articulate the implications of the Panopticon for society as a whole.

Frontispiece of Thomas Hobbes's *Leviathan*. London, 1651.
Reprints and new editions through the eighteenth and
nineteenth centuries included the allegory of the
homunculus on the title page.

The Great Seal of the United States, designed by Thomas Jefferson and Pierre Eugene du Simitiere, 1776. Modern version, as seen on the dollar bill.

For numerous reasons, many of which can no longer be traced, the implementation of this frontispiece ultimately foundered. For one, there were artistic challenges. In January 1791, Reveley recommended delivering the job "into the hands of some engraver used to engrave these things"[64]—a specialist who was difficult to come by in London, it would seem. Since the book's production process had become increasingly chaotic around that time, the delivery deadline extended yet again, Bentham lapsed into the subjunctive: "Had there been more time I would have added a

Declaration of the Rights of Man and of the Citizen, 1789–1790.

Frontispiece: a great gogle eye with rays round it representing the Panopticon out of triangle." Bentham had desperately wanted to see this aspect to completion, in order to use the book as an advertising brochure to accelerate the practical implementation of his Panopticon. There thus seems to have come a point at which Bentham abandoned the plan to illustrate his book, discarding images of the floorplan and cross sections along with the frontispiece, so as not to endanger the project as a whole. A further circumstance worth noting: had Reveley sent templates to the printer in Dublin—which can't be disproven with certainty—the frontispiece would likely have burned with the other illustrations. Counter to Bentham's intentions, the *Panopticon* thus appeared as a simple textbook—without the explanatory blueprints, and without the remarkable frontispiece.

GOD'S RATIONAL ORDER

Bentham's invocation of the Four Last Things, the Bible, and God was more than the legitimization of an unorthodox plan. It was a validity claim formulated for the political order at large, a declaration of an Enlightenment project slated to prepare the "body" of the people, in its totality, for freedom. All the more important, then, was the gaze on the godly image behind it all. In his 1687 publication, *Philosophiæ Naturalis Principia Mathematica*, Isaac Newton had revealed the mathematical order of the cosmic system, demonstrating that nature is based on consistent basic principles. There did appear to be a plan underlying divine creation, as had been assumed since the Middle Ages. Now, though, the existence, composition, and structure of this plan could be elucidated by scientific means. Newton's findings provided the first academic footing for the notion that God was a creator who adhered to principles of rationality. From that point on, the world itself could be considered the result and image of applied reason.

If creation could thus be understood as science, and humankind was made in the image of God, then the conceptual merging of these postulates yields a general shift in the conception of humanity. In the hundred years following Newton's work, this corollary became more defined, with disciples' obsession culminating in the eighteenth-century cult of Newton, whose members worshiped the scientist himself as a god. The French architect Etienne-Louis Boullée, for instance, designed a "Cenotaph for Newton" (1784),

Louis-Etienne Boulée: design for the so-called Cenotaph
for Sir Isaac Newton, 1784. Sectional drawing.

intended to serve as both a monumental mausoleum and
vivid symbol of a deciphered world order. Enthroned upon a
colossal plinth, the one-hundred-fifty-meter-tall sphere
represents a mathematical ideal form, the Pantheon of science that—as a precursor to the planetarium—captured
the very cosmos. The graphic arts, too, embraced the *topos*
of the "Newtonian man." William Blake, both poet and
painter, depicted "Newton as divine geometer" in 1795, thus
projecting onto the scientist an image common within medieval illuminated manuscripts, of "God as geometer." In
Blake's picture, Newton appears as a heroic nude sitting on
a rock, compass in hand, drafting a world plan on the paper
at his feet, a schematic drawing comprised of triangle, line,
and semicircle.[65]

William Blake, Newton as "divine geometer." Mirror-drawn
study for the painting, 1795. Pencil.

As an iconographic attribute in the visual arts, the compass belongs to the allegory of architecture, which was
connected to mathematics through the system of proportion from antiquity (Vitruvius) onward. "Geometer" can thus
be read as a synonym for "architect." This is further echoed
by the eighteenth-century Masonic interpretation that portrayed God as the "Supreme Architect of the Universe."[66]
With regard to the Panopticon, this line of thinking can help
explain the unusual eulogy Bentham the philosopher composed for architecture, a discipline foreign to him. He sees
architecture as capable of solving the fundamental questions

of society, because in it the ur-principle of rational creation takes on tangible form. From the divine architect to the blueprint for creating the world, the analogy can easily be applied to the human order: to the "building politic," which, when leveled against Hobbes, replaces the traditional metaphor of the "body politic." Yet again, Bentham's inspection principle invites interpretation as a state model[67]—girded by the fact that it did not stop at the emblematic antithesis to Hobbes. Bentham sought this synthesis, the dissolution of the allegorical predecessor through the annexation (in the truest sense) of its symbolic strategy. "The lodge is the heart, which gives life and motion to this artificial body."[68] Or, in technical terms: the inspector at the eye of the Panopticon sets the wheels of education in motion. Bentham thus reserved for himself both possible metaphors of the state—"building" and "body"—and occupied every politically symbolic semantic field available. Only in this way could he surpass the power of Hobbes's widely disseminated cipher.

Architecture as creation—creation as science. Bentham, too, joined the artists and intellectuals dedicated to Newton's legacy. "[All] the great men of the Enlightenment were in search for the organon of morals which should repeat the physical triumphs of Newton," wrote John Dewey in 1910, and continued: "Bentham notes that physics has had its Bacon and Newton; that morals has had its Bacon in Helvétius, but still awaits its Newton; and he leaves us in no doubt that at the moment of writing he was ready, modestly but firmly, to fill the waiting niche with its missing."[69] A self-described "Newton of moral philosophy,"[70] Bentham

Allegory of architecture. Frontispiece of Leon Christoph Sturm and Aegidius Strauch's *Tabulae sinuum tangentium logarithmorum et per universam mathesin*. Amsterdam, 1700.

"God as geometer." Frontispiece of the *Bible moralisé,
Codex Vindobonensis 2554* (Austrian National Library).
France, ca. 1250.

worked on applying scientific findings to human nature. He borrowed Newton's model of the universe, based in part on the principle of push and pull between physical bodies, and projected this notion onto the human soul. According to Bentham, two rival, contradictory forces prevail, pushing and pulling at each other, alternating in intensity and impact, tangibly quantifiable in terms of their cause: pleasure and pain. The human drive toward pleasure is as inherent as gravitational force on Earth. Humans are naturally repulsed by pain. Bentham first published this thesis—the so-called Principle of Utility—in the *Introduction to the Principles of Morals and Legislation*, which appeared almost concurrently with the revised *Panopticon*. The definition reads:

> Nature has placed mankind under the governance of two sovereign masters, pain and pleasure. It is for them alone to point out what we ought to do, as well as to determine what we shall do. On the one hand the standard of right and wrong, on the other the chain of causes and effects, are fastened to their throne. They govern us in all we do, in all we say, in all we think: every effort we make to throw off our subjection, will serve but to demonstrate and confirm it. In words a man may pretend to abjure their empire: but in reality he will remain subject to it all the while. The principle of utility recognises this subjection, and assumes it for the foundation of that system, the object of which is to rear the fabric of felicity by the hands of reason and of law. Systems which attempt to question it, deal in sounds

instead of sense, in caprice instead of reason, in dark-ness instead of light.[71]

Bentham—again, as an enlightened disciple of New-ton's—assumed that his model of moral powers enjoyed universal validity. The "social gravitation principle," in which the individual appears as a "social atom,"[72] existed inde-pendently of cultural influence or place of residence, given the "equality and immutability of human nature." Bentham's scientific, almost technocratic view of the soul culminated in his "felicific calculus," which was intended to measure and catalog human happiness.[73] The "measurements" of emo-tional reactions were sorted and assigned spots within a register of twelve fundamental types of pain and fourteen fundamental types of pleasure. These data could be ana-lyzed to reveal the "intensity and duration" of an emotion and to predict the likelihood of its appearance, possible side effects, and the number of people sharing in the pleasure. Bentham imagined creating these emotions in a laboratory setting, as it were, one that seems a blend of scientific experiment and sociological field study:

> To take an exact account then of the general tendency of any act, by which the interests of a community are affected, proceed as follows. Begin with any one person of those whose interests seem most immediately to be affected by it: and take an account,
>
> 1. Of the value of each distinguishable pleasure which appears to be produced by it in the first instance.

2. Of the value of each pain which appears to be produced by it in the first instance.

3. Of the value of each pleasure which appears to be produced by it after the first. This constitutes the fecundity of the first pleasure and the impurity of the first pain.

4. Of the value of each pain which appears to be produced by it after the first. This constitutes the fecundity of the first pain, and the impurity of the first pleasure.

5. Sum up all the values of all the pleasures on the one side, and those of all the pains on the other. The balance, if it be on the side of pleasure, will give the good tendency of the act upon the whole, with respect to the interests of that individual person; if on the side of pain, the bad tendency of it upon the whole. ...[74]

Under what other conditions, in what other place, can one better imagine these human explorations into increasing pleasure than in the Panopticon? The *Introduction* reads like a handbook for the inspection house, describing the structure, character, and objective of an experiment for which Bentham's Panopticon provides the perfect laboratory. From the center of the structure, the overseer can directly monitor the effects of disciplinary measures implemented on the delinquents. The felicific calculus is measured in each cell and tabulated. This measure of pleasure is used to assess how far an inmate had progressed along the desired route toward maturity. The destiny of freedom becomes rationally tangible, unsullied by subjective mistakes in judgment by the "management," thereby truly allowing every person to become the "architect of one's own fortune" unimpeded.

The analogy to Newton presents itself once more, as he performed his groundbreaking experiments with the help of two optical instruments. Using a prism, he broke a beam of white light into its spectral colors. And with a "reflecting

Isaac Newton, telescope design from the *Philosophical Transactions*, 1672.

telescope" he had developed himself, he observed planetary movement. The motifs of "light," "prism," "beam," and "observation," as well as perception through the "noblest sense" (Goethe)[75]—the eye—also occupy a key place in Bentham's applied moral philosophy, which emphasized the planned frontispiece in its double meaning: beams of light pour from the eye of God to the walls of the enclosing triangle, whose basic geometric form can be interpreted as the "prism" of the inspection principle. In other words, with the help of applied science (philosophy), one is equipped to decipher divine creation to its very crowning instance— one's own self.

Bentham's reciprocal reflections of meaning and motif ultimately join in a rhetorical vanishing point, the programmatic title of the *Inspection House*. The term "Panopticon" does not belong in philosophy. It is borrowed from the natural sciences.[76] It describes an instrument that could be either telescope or prism, the "all-seeing," divinely wise moral philosophical equivalent to those tools that guided Newton to his discoveries. Rather than probing the skies, Bentham simply turns the telescope around and fixes it on the viewer. In this way, the Panopticon becomes a key to wisdom. It is Bentham's universal instrument for deciphering humans, the soul, and the laws of the soul—for the benefit of all.

CURIOSITY (EVEN BETTER THAN THE REAL THING)

In 1787, while Bentham was active in Krychaw, the painter Robert Barker submitted to the English patent office a proposal outlining an idea remarkably similar to the Panopticon. At the center of a circular hall was a viewing platform, from which visitors could admire large-format, thematic cycloramas mounted on the building's circular walls. Barker gave the patent a Greek name meaning, roughly, "all sight." In 1792, one year after Bentham's *Panopticon* was published, Barker opened the first "panorama" in London's Leicester Square. The content on display was largely banal. Illustrated histories, dramatized current events, landscapes, cityscapes, perhaps the view from a rooftop, reflected naturalistically. Barker's suggestive game with the technical imitation of reality, the visitors' unbounded-bounded view, the entrenched sense of "to see and be seen"—he truly had his finger on the pulse of the day. The very first hype of a veritable entertainment industry made the painter a rich man.

Stephan Oettermann described the panorama as "a machine, in which the sovereignty of the bourgeois gaze is at once learned and exalted, an instrument for the liberation and the renewed imprisonment of the gaze."[77] This formulation—remarkably similar to Foucault's exegesis of Bentham—immediately suggests the close kinship between "panorama" and "Panopticon." In fact, Bentham was well aware of his contemporaries' curiosity. He wanted to take advantage of it, and did so in welcoming viewers to the Panopticon for a special entertainment program:

Among my undivulged instruments of amusement and good morals for the prisoners in Panopticon one was singing in chorus: for audience, volunteer visitors in the Central Lodge. Tune 1. Malbrook, Coda to the song, "Our worthy Governor." Stanza, reciting in verse all the good things he stood engaged to do for them, and stating them as done. This, in so far as done, would be just eulogy; in so far left undone, merited satire and accusation before all the world. Tune 2. Another pretty melody, and almost as simple—"Drink and set your hearts at rest: / Of a bad bargain make the best." Words the same, except, that instead of drink, in stanza 1, work; stanza 2, learn; in stanza 3, sing.[78]

Although it would appear as though consumer culture and the inspection principle were identical twins, indistinguishable in their optically centered design, the objective of each is distinct. If Bentham set out to parade the inmates in front of the public, his aim was not to expose those individuals. Masks were worn to protect the delinquents' identity, as in ancient Greek theater—a reference to the mythical dramas and fates that found themselves repeated here, in the "moral institute" of the Panopticon.[79] Other institutions such as Bedlam, the storied hospital in London that served as a hybrid psychiatric unit and poor law infirmary, were known to showcase madmen, murderers, and cripples for an entrance fee, but Bentham rejected the "freak show."[80] His renditions of the modern-day *Ecce homo* were intended to touch the soul and intellect of the audience, teaching those viewers by means of catharsis. This meant having to

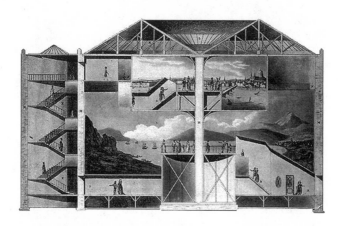

Panorama in Leicester Square, London, 1792. Design and execution: Robert Barker. Sectional drawing.

stage everyday life in prison (itself rather mundane) and overinflate it to become an edifying drama about reform, reason, and economy—an allegorical piece about human potential and the return to a happier society. Only it wasn't a "theatrical performance" being presented, but reality itself.

Theatrical responses to aspects of reality helped form the repertoire of a time that did not distinguish public from private, phenomenon from symbol, in the modern sense. In Bath, for instance, passersby observed spa visitors bathing every day. Bodily cleansing and regeneration were (also) symbols of moral edification. Executions (whether performed by the old state or mutinous masses), impaled heads, and torn-out hearts were never solely political acts; instead, they served as moral examples, which the

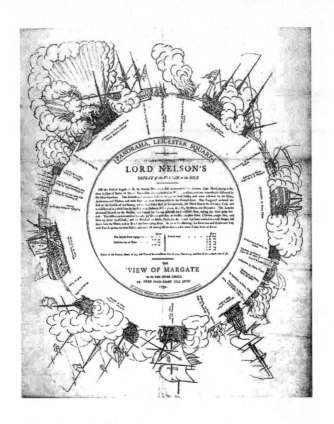

Program from the panorama in Leicester Square. London, 1799.

propagandistic brochures of the time reflected, at times pointedly, at times exhaustively.[81] It was not until the late eighteenth century that this immediacy, which was multifaceted in significance, became sublimated. Emotional distance and control gradually became defining elements

THE PANOPTICON

of the bourgeois disposition. This development led to the immoralizing of spectacle, to its banishment to the private sphere. And at its end is pure consumption. The panorama had already reduced the manifold connotations of "showing" by the morally instructive "demonstrating."[82] What remained was simple "presenting," the cultural added value of which no longer includes a gain in moral knowledge; instead, that gain can be found in education and formation and perfecting the artistic-technical handling of the subject.

Bentham countered this burgeoning consumerism with the desire for edification. The theater also seemed to him a fitting analogy, given his belief that punishment could be instructive and influential only when merely played, rather

King's Bath in Bath, 1672. Contemporary engraving of bathers and eager spectators.

than when meted out. The psychological power of simulation (Bentham credited the Spanish Inquisition as his model) is based on imagination. It constructs a mental threat of such insistence that adherence to the law results almost necessarily. And after one visit to the Panopticon, this mental terror—a thrill unlike any mass spectacle—was intended to leave a pedagogical mark on the population:

> Here, to one room, you have Inspectors by thousands. Is it possible that a national Penitentiary-House of this kind should be more at a loss for visitors than the lions, the wax-work, or the tomb? Of the 25,000 individuals born annually in London, I want but one of a hundred, and him but once in his life, without reckoning country visitors. Call it a spectacle for youth, and for youth only:—Youth, however, do not go to spectacles alone.[83]

It's here that the Potemkin lessons that served as the foundation for the Panopticon come to full fruition: truths (or lies) are imbued with a moral dimension through media presentation and dramatic exaggeration. Bentham was aware that nothing short of a creative impresario could shape the Panopticon into the wide-reaching instrument of reform he envisioned. And who was more obvious a candidate than himself?

> Let me construct a prison on this model and I am willing to become the gaoler of it; you will see ... that this gaoler desires no salary and will cost nothing to the nation. The more I consider the subject, the more I am convinced, that this is one of the projects, the execution of which should be left in the hands of the inventor.[84]

THE PANOPTICON

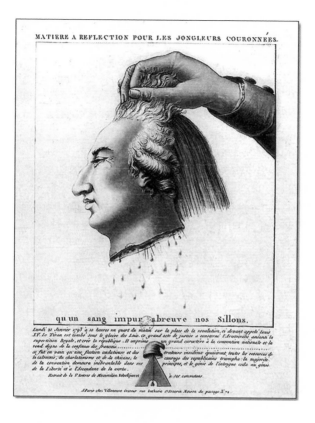

Handbill advertising the execution of King Louis XVI in today's Place de la Concorde in Paris, January 1793, with the admonition to "reflect."

The more deeply we peer into the eye of the Panopticon, the more clearly the London-born philosopher gazes back. He wears Biedermeier garb, a massive hat on his head and walking stick in hand, and he sits in a chair, waiting: Jeremy Bentham, the sole legitimate guardian of the inspection principle, and simultaneously its most tenacious marketer. He devoted himself to this project as to no other throughout his life, filling what must have been thousands of pages of manuscript; he concocted new variations, drafted pamphlets, exposés, and letters, and led discussions with the aim of convincing his fellow human beings of the necessity of this idea. The failure of the Millbank penitentiary, which would have provided the perfect setting in which to prove the validity of the felicific calculus, did not deter him. Even later perversions, from solitary confinement to concentration camps, may not have been enough to hinder his continued attempts. The "radical fool" did not pause to consider that the laws of this supposed cosmos of truth might exist only in his mind. To the bitter end, he fought back against the suggestion that the Panopticon was nothing more than a utopia.

THE AUTO-ICON

Jeremy Bentham's Auto-Icon, produced 1832–1833.
Modern presentation without cabinet.

IN THE SERVICE OF SCIENCE

Toward the end of his life, Jeremy Bentham abandoned his obsessive fight for the Panopticon. A new experiment took its place, a second attempt to evaluate utilitarian theories, which he outlined in his final essay, "Auto-Icon, or Farther Uses of the Dead to the Living." By 1769, at the age of twenty-two, Bentham had already decided to bequeath his body to science, to compensate—as a dead man—for the opportunities to do good he may have missed in life.[1] The fulfillment of this childish prophesy stared the aged Bentham in the face daily. The chance to succeed Montesquieu had been refused him. Bentham hadn't written the constitution for any states. Although his total writings comprised nothing less than the foundation for a utilitarian world order—an "all-comprehensive Code (or say, in one word, of my Pannomion)"[2]—and although he created a "science of legislation" to complement the "science of morals," he never enjoyed a decisive breakthrough. For years, Bentham had contacted reform-friendly governments around the world, had offered his services in North and South America, Russia, and Europe. And when he finally was hired to author a liberal Portuguese constitution in 1821, he spread himself so thin that he was ultimately unable to present a final product. To truly become "legislator of the world," an honorary title bestowed upon Bentham by his students and disciples, would remain little more than a dream of his.[3]

England forever maintained a reserved stance toward his ideas. The attempts at prison reform soon lost momentum;

the establishment of the model prison at Pentonville in 1842 marked the beginning of the grim chapter of brutal Victorian corrections. Not even the shipment of prisoners to Australia would end until 1868. Suffrage laws continued to block most of the population from voting. Moreover, society as a whole was further from an awakening than ever before. Napoleon, the inventor and founder of a modern European civil code, died a warmonger on Saint Helena in 1821, vanquished by the English, whose successes abroad allowed them to defend the old order at home. After a sixty-year reign, Bentham's archenemy George III was succeeded by George IV (1820), who was followed by William IV (1830) and then Victoria (1837). Restoration swept through all of Europe. Censorship truncated human rights. The aristocracy asserted power and influence, side by side with the burgeoning bourgeoisie. The economy and the state remained closely intertwined, but capitalism had taken on colossal dimensions. A new lower class emerged in the face of industrial magnates' astronomical fortunes. Farmers had given way to factory workers, or "paupers," earning starvation wages. The ideal of economic liberalism proposed by Adam Smith and espoused by Bentham and his students had remained little more than a dream. The time was ripe to do good, and the philosopher hoped for a final attempt at it in death: "Having from my earliest youth devoted my mental faculties to the service of mankind what remains for me is to devote my body to that same purpose."[4]

Bentham pondered the topic without regard to dogma, traditions, customs, or established law. He avoided any false pity by applying his theses to himself. He utterly

THE AUTO-ICON

ignored the question of the soul, which historically had been closely tied to metaphysics. He soberly narrowed his focus on the human body and, in a manner unprecedented in philosophy, viewed it as "material."[5] For one, traditional burial regulations appeared profoundly wrong from a utilitarian perspective. The handling of corpses was required by law for hygienic and religious reasons, and by force of habit. This made profiteers of the "undertakers, solicitors, [and] priests."[6] Furthermore, it blocked the economically sensible utilization of the body. To circumvent the prescribed institutional path—that is, to secure the future corpse for "useful" purposes—Bentham declared his body an inheritance. He bequeathed it to his friend Southwood Smith, a surgeon, and stipulated that Smith perform a ceremonial autopsy. Bentham's body was (initially) slated to serve medical research.

Bentham's act was an affront against his own time. The body—vessel of the soul, a piece of Creation in the likeness of the Creator—was a holy entity. Its destruction was an act of blasphemy by proxy. The law included a single exception, also the result of occidental conventions of thought and action based on the adaptation of Christian cults of image. This exception applied to the bodies of murderers. Following the Murder Act of 1752, their bodies were explicitly earmarked for anatomical study, because vivisection promised mutilation of the face—a sentence greater than death. (Even anatomists themselves insisted on Christian burials, their bodies untouched.)[7]

In 1824, Southwood Smith lodged the first objection to the established regulations. His pamphlet "Use of the Dead

William Hogarth, *The Reward of Cruelty*, 1751. The height of human barbarism: vivisection of a murderer in an anatomical theater.

THE AUTO-ICON

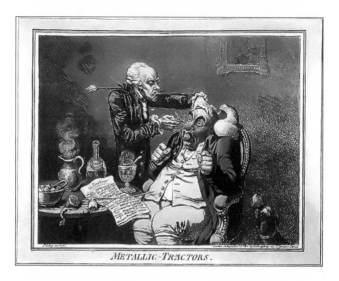

A quack at work. Caricature by Thomas Rowlandson, ca. 1815.

to the Living," a direct precursor to Bentham's own contemplations, demonstrated concisely that without foundational anatomical research, the medical field would remain unable to meet contemporary scientific standards:

> Disease, which it is the object of these arts to prevent and to cure, is denoted by disordered function: disordered function cannot be understood without a knowledge of healthy function; healthy function cannot be understood without a knowledge of structure; structure cannot be understood unless it is examined.[8]

By the late eighteenth century, doctors in London had only just won the battle with barbers, whose guild had traditionally been responsible for the dissection of living and dead. In 1783, Doctor John Hunter opened an institute of anatomy with attached museum in Leicester Square. The Company of Surgeons, renamed the Royal College of Surgeons in 1802, campaigned vehemently for doctors to hold the medical monopoly. Uniform hygienic standards were to replace the charlatan practices of cupping and bloodletting visited upon the lower classes by barber surgeons at the fair. At the same time, widespread misconceptions had to be dispelled, such as the practice of "mesmerism," the use of magnets to alter the nerves, which was well received throughout Europe. This shift could only occur through serious research and practical experience. A societal dimension was thus always inherent to such full-throated declarations of professional ethics as Southwood Smith's pamphlet. In addition to providing medical care to society's poorest, the required conversion of poor houses and general hospitals into research facilities also enabled medical training on living bodies: "If the dead bodies of the poor are not appropriated to this use, their living bodies will and must be." Smith thus invoked the cornerstone of Bentham's belief system: exemplary social reform built on a utilitarian foundation.

In 1828, a criminal case revealed the heart of the medical dilemma. Two Irishmen, William Burke and William Hare, had for months supplied the Edinburgh surgery with cadavers, which were in short supply; they were delivering, however, not the bodies of murderers but of murder victims. The duo initially exhumed graves (earning them the moniker "resurrectionists"), then moved on to getting petty thieves drunk and suffocating them with pillows. By the end, Burke and Hare were systematically combing the city for fair game, killing runaways and lunatics. Countless cadavers later, the police caught up with them. Burke's execution in January 1829 drew a crowd of thirty thousand eager spectators. At the public dissection of his body shortly thereafter, the angry mob is reported to have tried to destroy the Edinburgh medical facility; its director, Dr. Robert Knox, was recognized as the actual instigator in the incidents.[9]

Execution & Confession of BURKE.
On Wednesday, January, 28th, 1829, for the West Port Murders, at Edinburgh,

Handbill advertising the execution of the "body snatcher" William Burke. Edinburgh, January 1829.

New ordinances to prevent grave robbery now allowed for triple coffins, patented iron tubs (with springs to prevent the lid from being opened), and multiple rows of nails.[10] Copycat criminals and the material costs carried by families further heightened the hysteria surrounding the "body snatchers" (Robert Louis Stevenson), such that they may have helped facilitate Bentham's dying wishes. Just days after the philosopher's death, Parliament passed a bill, promoted by those in Bentham's circle, to reform the Murder Act. Southwood Smith therefore required special permission to perform the vivisection. The procedure provided the opportunity to illustrate a utilitarian paradox Bentham would often vary: under certain circumstances, a small wrong could prevent greater wrongs and thus contribute to human happiness. The mutilation of the philosopher's cadaver, while officially a "wrong," served as an example for future cadaver donations; this then made it possible to cover long-term surgical needs, prevent further grave robbery, and most importantly, stimulate research and discovery.

FAITH WITHOUT RELIGION

Bentham died in London on June 6, 1832, at the age of eighty-four. On June 8, Southwood Smith invited the public to the Webb Street School of Anatomy.[11] A lecture planned for June 11 at the same location would elucidate the significance of this groundbreaking symbolic deed: death, lecture, and vivisection were the first three acts of the dramatic execution of Bentham's will. Bentham, who had wished to inhabit the eye of the Panopticon as guardian of the inspection principle, now assumed his place in the center of the anatomical theater. The auditorium transformed into an ethics institute. An eyewitness described the event:

> None who were present can ever forget that impressive scene. The room (the lecture-room of the Webb Street School of Anatomy) is small and circular, with no window but a central skylight, and capable of containing about three hundred persons. It was filled, with the exception of a class of medical students and some eminent members of that profession, by friends, disciples, and admirers of the deceased philosopher, comprising many men celebrated for literary talent, scientific research, and political activity.[12]

As master of ceremonies for his own vivisection, Bentham had carefully considered the mix of spectators. Medical lectures were regularly announced and discussed in popular newspapers.[13] The illustrious circle of family and friends in attendance piqued further interest, and as eye witnesses they were also expected to ratify the "usefulness" of the scheduled act. Without a doubt, this was a community gathered to profess their utilitarian faith. Southwood Smith paid effusive tribute to Bentham's character. He enumerated his accomplishments as a political thinker. Then he quoted from the foundational text of his political worldview—the *Introduction to the Principles of Morals and Legislation*—selecting the key introductory lines from the "Principle of Utility." Under these circumstances, the words must have taken on the quality of prayer: "Nature has placed mankind under the governance of two sovereign masters, *pain* and *pleasure*. It is for them alone to point out what we ought to do."

> The corpse was on the table in the middle of the room, directly under the light, clothed in a night-dress, with only the head and hands exposed. There was no rigidity in the features, but an expression of placid dignity and benevolence.

The room itself underscored the holiness of the cere-mony. The monumental form of the anatomical theater reflected doctors' status and heralded their search for the seed of creation, for God's work and his likeness. Jacques Gondoin's lecture hall at the École de Chirurgie in Paris (1769–1775) was the first building formulated in this fash-ion, the hall interpreted as a halved pantheon crowned with a cupula opening to the skies.[14] Temples of reason such as this immersed the doctors' work in a sacred aura. Under the cupula of the Webb Street School of Anatomy—a smaller

Pl. XXIX.

Auditorium at the École de Médicine, Paris. Designed by Jacques Gondoin, 1769–1775. Contemporary copper engraving from Gondoin's publication, *Description des Écoles de Chirurgie* (Paris, 1780).

successor of the Parisian model—and the heavens above, lay the inventor of the Panopticon, related in its own way to the Pantheon and anatomical theaters. Myriad motifs permeated the space. The tension grew as in a gothic novel. When Southwood Smith finally started the procedure, a thunderstorm broke out. The ceremony

> was at times rendered almost vital by the reflection of the lightning playing over them; for a storm arose just as the lecturer commenced, and the profound silence in which he was listened to was broken and only broken by loud peals of thunder, which continued to roll at intervals throughout the delivery of his most appropriate and often affecting address.

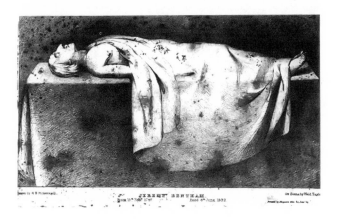

The deceased Jeremy Bentham on the dissecting table. Frontispiece of Southwood Smith's publication, *A Lecture Delivered Over the Remains of Jeremy Bentham, Esq.* (London, 1832).

THE AUTO-ICON

One can assume that the report intentionally lends the scene its mood, especially considering weather patterns in London, where summer thunderstorms are in no way uncommon and would not otherwise warrant mention. However, the fact that Southwood Smith is said to have spoken "with a clear unfaltering voice, but with a face as white as that of the dead philosopher before him" as the entire building "shook"[15] shows that something else was at play: natural phenomena that occur on command are religious spectacles.

Matthew 27: 50–53 depicts the end of the Savior: "Jesus, when he had cried again with a loud voice, yielded up the ghost. / And, behold, the veil of the temple was rent in twain from the top to the bottom; and the earth did quake, and the rocks rent; / And the graves were opened; and many bodies of the saints which slept arose, / And came out of the graves after his resurrection, and went into the holy city, and appeared unto many."[16] In a foreshadowing of Judgment Day, God greets the crucifixion of his son with a show of omnipotence; He buffets the completed sacrifice, imbuing the key moment of Christian doctrine with metaphysical heft. From this point, the revelation is fulfilled: after death shall come resurrection. First, though, come discovery and knowledge. Matthew leaves no doubt as to the effect of God's sign on the people: "Now when the centurion, and they that were with him, watching Jesus, saw the earthquake, and those things that were done, they feared greatly, saying, Truly this was the Son of God." The truth was made manifest.

Bentham's vivisection (with media coverage) unfurls as an analogue to the biblical scene, albeit with inverse intentions, skewed motives, and a different reason for the heavens' furious interjection: God revolts against His exposure through the human spirit, which has devoted itself—against His will—to knowledge (and therefore temptation) since the days in paradise. By means of Bentham's body (the Eucharist!), Smith celebrates metaphysics' final conquest. Materialism and reason triumph and religious dogma founders, proven useless and outdated. In the modern age, it is none other than the doctor who rips the dead from their graves. A simultaneous act of enlightenment and rebellion, for which the philosopher fought for years, and in which his aversion to religion and church had reached immeasurable heights:

> Religion is an engine, invented by corruptionists, at the command of tyrants, for the manufactory of dupes.[17]

Bentham-Antichrist: the revelation fulfilled the moment the surgeon's scalpel penetrated his flesh. "By this act he carries by his own personal example, the great practicle principle, for the development and enforcement of which he has raised to himself an immortal name."[18] A reporter at the *Monthly Repository* considered it "a worthy close of the personal career of the great philanthropist and philosopher," which served as the apotheosis for true heroes:

> Never did corpse of hero on the battlefield, with his martial cloak around him, or funeral obsequies chanted by stoled and mitred priests in Gothic aisles, excite such emotions as the stern simplicity of that hour in which

THE AUTO-ICON

the principle of utility triumphed over the imagination and the heart.

As witnessed by students, descendants, and those eager to learn, Bentham became one with his teachings. In place of those for whom he wanted to do good, he entered the infinite kingdom of scientific reason. From that point forward, he was no longer simply the founder of utilitarianism but the very proof of its validity.

MĀORI AND PHYSIOGNOMISTS

After the execution of the first three acts of Bentham's dying wishes came the next step. Southwood Smith assembled the dissected parts of Bentham's body, stiffened the skeleton, dressed it, and arranged it as a living portrait, a so-called Auto-Icon. Straw and cloth were fashioned to provide corporeal volume around the bones and the heart was placed in a glass jar, but Bentham had devised a special procedure for his head after its removal from his torso. It was to be prepared according to the drying methods employed by the Māori of New Zealand to create *mokomokai*, or preserved heads. The cultural practice, first described in Captain James Cook's account of exploring the South Seas, had become known to the wider public in London through the 1820 visit of Hongi Hika, a Christianized Māori intermediary enlisted to promote cultural exchange between indigenous peoples and colonists, who became a society favorite. On the return voyage to New Zealand, Hongi Hika traded gifts from King George for new types of firearms, called his tribe into battle, and unleashed an apocalyptic bloodbath on their rivals. Following each victory, the enemy heads were dried en masse and traded for more weapons. Scores of *mokomokai* thus made their way to England, where they were showcased, acquired by museums, and gathered by collectors, even following the 1831 trade prohibition.[19]

Bentham was by no means fazed by either the massacre England had indirectly prompted or the ritualized cruelty. He appraised the trophies—dismissively dubbed "baked heads"—as technical innovations and recognized their potential for his own plans. He enthusiastically praised the "savage ingenuity." An 1824 draft of his will was the first to contain the score of his wishes: first, to see the corpse as an inheritance (for "my dear friend Dr. Armstrong" at the time, as he had not yet met Southwood Smith); second, to make a scientific-political example of the vivisection; and third, to put forward the Auto-Icon as a lasting emblem.[20] According to legend, Bentham carried around the glass eyes intended for the Auto-Icon in his pocket in his final years. (Supposed) attempts at dehydrating body parts in his home oven are said to have yielded satisfactory results. Bentham believed the *mokomokai* process would discolor facial traits and produce a parchment- or mummy-like appearance (which could be corrected with paint), while maintaining the physiognomy. For a denizen of the eighteenth century, who believed that facial lines were an expression of personality and a reflection of the soul, this was the deciding factor. Bentham defined "a man who is his own image": to preserve his "identity," the Auto-Icon had to correspond exactly to the living man, beyond his death.[21]

But Southwood Smith botched the job.[22] He sprinkled sulfuric acid onto the head, and in doing so docked Bentham's nose. He used an air pump to aid dehydration, which caused the skin to shrivel. Bentham's face appeared melted, the physiognomy destroyed. In spring 1833, Smith commissioned a replacement head of wax, for which he likely enlisted the Frenchman Jacques Talrich, a trained doctor who created anatomical instructional materials out of wax

The English Colonel H. G. Robley, following dispatch to
New Zealand, poses in front of his collection of
mokomokai. Photograph, ca. 1900.

and lived in London in the early 1830s.[23] In addition to studying painted and drawn portraits, Talrich used two works
crafted by the sculptor David d'Angers during Bentham's
1825 visit to Paris as a template: a marble bust that had
been in Bentham's private collection since 1828, and a
medal displaying both the philosopher's profile in relief and
his handwritten signature. The work was part of a prodi-
gious art project comprising over five hundred medals

David d'Angers (Pierre Jean David), medal depicting
Johann Wolfgang von Goethe, 1829.

depicting people of note, whom d'Angers viewed as the
building blocks of an intellectual pantheon.

D'Angers reserved a certain scientific pretense for his
renderings, based on the teachings of phrenology (the connection between character and skull shape), physiognomy
(the connection between character and facial features and
proportions), and graphology (the connection between
character and handwriting). His medal of Goethe, along with
his famous plaster bust of the poet (Paris, Musée d'Orsay)
created in 1829 in Weimar, illustrates the approach: since

David d'Angers (Pierre Jean David), bust of Jeremy
Bentham, 1825. Today housed at University College
London.

contemporary theories emphasized prominent physical features as the sign of an individual's intellect and character,
d'Angers enhanced those supposed features of genius (high
forehead, distinctive nose, flowing tresses) to such a degree
that the result eclipsed the individual's actual appearance.
This primacy of artistic stylization on a "scientific" basis also
applied to the bust of Bentham—and therefore to the wax

THE AUTO-ICON

head modeled after it for the Auto-Icon. The fact that Talrich's completed work, trimmed with the philosopher's real hair, was so well-received by contemporaries—"so perfect, that it seems alive"[24]—was based less on true similarity in external appearance than on the formal ardor required—and at the time, even desired—in depicting extraordinary intellectual capacity. Realism, or even naturalism, was a concept foreign to this art. Strictly speaking, Bentham's original idea for the Auto-Icon as "a man who is his own image" was thus a failure.

At the end of the production process, Southwood Smith positioned the Auto-Icon, dressed in its best suit, on a chair, as if it had just returned home after its daily stroll. He placed Bentham's real, disfigured head on a plate between his slippered feet. Its power as a memorial was tempered by its private bearing. It was not placed on a pedestal, conjuring grandeur and distance. The Auto-Icon lacked the characteristics espoused by exaggerated plaques, as echoed in some accounts of Bentham in his later years:

> His apparel hung loosely about him, and consisted chiefly of a grey coat, light breeches, and white woollen stockings, hanging loosely about his legs; whilst his venerable locks, which floated over the collar and down his back, were surmounted by a straw hat of most grotesque and indescribable shape, communicating to his appearance a strong contrast to the quietude and sobriety of his general aspect. He wended round the walks of his garden at a pace somewhat faster than a walk, but not so quick as a trot.[25]

Bentham managed, despite his approaching death, to remain a part of the society he had often hosted at dinners. The mahogany cabinet housing the Auto-Icon, built with glass doors according to Bentham's design, thus served a practical purpose: it made "Bentham" mobile. In his will, he encouraged friends and students to meet regularly "at a club in commemoration of my birth and death." In fact, he wished to join in these gatherings:

> My desire is, that in that case order may be taken by my executor, for such my skeleton seated in an appropriate chair, to be placed, on the occasion of any such meeting, at one end of the table, after the manner in which at a public meeting a chairman is commonly seated.[26]

The Auto-Icon allowed the utilitarian initiation ritual at the Webb Street School of Anatomy to be reprised ad infinitum: with new visitors (including guests such as Charles Dickens), students, and disciples of the philosophical doctrine, and personally presided over by its founder. Along these very lines, Southwood Smith exhibited "Bentham" in the mahogany cabinet in his practice in London's Bloomsbury neighborhood, and frequently brought him along to social events, parties, and discussions. This ritual continued, albeit with some interruptions, until "Bentham" arrived at University College London in the mid-nineteenth century, following a stopover in a museum. His ability to travel from his current location in the South Cloisters of the main building of UCL, however, is hindered by limited accessibility.

Jeremy Bentham's Auto-Icon. Detail of the wax head
crafted by Jacques Talrich, 1832.

Most recently in 2006, his participation in an international
conference on utilitarianism was limited to presiding over
the speakers' dinner, which was also moved to a room on
the same floor.[27]

THE PHILOSOPHER AS WORLD MODEL

From the first, English society was unruffled by Bentham's idea, which he had delivered as an ultimatum. The scandal was quickly defused by a long-standing social mechanism for normalizing the bizarre: Bentham joined the ranks of "eccentrics," a special type of individualist who had emerged in the eighteenth century from the leveled society of aristocracy and elevated bourgeoisie. Among Bentham's contemporaries were a considerable number of hypernervous characters whose purpose in life was to be different.[28] John Mytton, for instance, outdid the sartorial enthusiast "Beau" Brummell through his accumulation of three thousand shirts, one thousand hats, seven hundred pairs of shoes, and one hundred fifty pairs of jodhpurs. He fed his two thousand dogs steak and champagne and clad his eighty cats in livery. And nearly every time he went out riding, he made an effort to kill himself. John Fuller, on the other hand, a parliamentarian and proponent of natural sciences and the arts, appeared to possess a spiritual kinship to Prince Pückler-Muskau. He constructed a range of bizarre monuments, pavilions, and follies on his estate. And finally, the painter-poet William Blake loved to recite passages from John Milton's *Paradise Lost* in his garden, and, along with his wife, slip into the roles of Adam and Eve—naked.

The two-volume compendium *English Eccentrics and Eccentricities* (1866) enumerates over one hundred personalities and incidents, and describes prominent examples of spendthrifts, philanthropists, religious fanatics,

THE AUTO-ICON

opium-eaters, and "radicals"; alongside Bentham, the list also included the rebellious William Beckford with his tirade against King George III. Many of these personalities made use of their impending death for eccentric positioning. Cryptic epitaphs, peculiar bequests, and unexpected inheritances were part of the standard repertoire. Coffins—self-constructed, lovingly designed—were installed in the home as a wardrobe or wine rack during the individual's lifetime. Memorial cults existed that far surpassed opulent family tombs. And there are absurd burial specifications. In 1800, for instance, General Labeliere was buried on a hill between London and Brighton, his body lowered vertically into the ground, headfirst. He wanted to be prepared: in case "the world was turned topsy-turvy, it was fit that he should be so buried that he might be right at last."[29] Like Bentham, he needed to do this without church approval.

"A man perfect in his way, and beautifully unfit for walking in the way of any other man."[30] This definition of the eccentric, which could also serve as an edict of tolerance, was penned by the poet Algernon Charles Swinburne with regard to William Blake. Every eccentric had to discover his own personal quirk, as a finely contrived medium for social distinction. This was a very specific type of challenge. Thanks to the Auto-Icon, Bentham had clearly passed this test with flying colors. The adoring cult of the weird, however, stripped his project of its philosophical point. Bentham had not intended to become a curiosity. He had wanted to perpetuate the exemplary morality of vivisection. The visual death for science was to be answered by visual resurrection.

He sought to appeal to observers. The Auto-Icon was an invitation to imitate life according to the principle of utility. It was the final puzzle piece in Bentham's sweeping project of social reform, and as such, it was trained on eternity.

Southwood Smith did not pass the memento on to a museum, but installed it in his own chambers, because Bentham had contended that the moral influence of any Auto-Icon would develop best amid those who survived the deceased. The argument is plausible when considered in the context of curio and natural history collections, the *Kunstkammern* or "cabinets of curiosities" that had been filled with treasures from church or royal troves from the sixteenth century onward.[31] In a cabinet of curiosities—an antecedent to the modern museum laid out according to "*Artificialia*," "*Naturalia*," or "*Exotica*"—objects of motley provenance were displayed together, in contrast to later collections' scientific and systematic arrangement. Morphological criteria were deciding factors, but most important was the nod to the collector as a gentleman of moral integrity and political acumen. Viewed holistically, these collections of nuts, ostrich eggs, turnery, whale bones, automatons, gemstones, and hunting trophies could each serve as a miniaturized model of the universe. Ancestral portrait galleries often attached to the cabinet of curiosities extended this cosmic symbolism directly to the collector himself. There are several analogies between the Auto-Icon and cabinets of curiosities: taxidermied creatures, inanimate objects imitating life (automatons, the portable Auto-Icon), the reference to the collector's political or moral intentions, the attempt to craft an explanation of the world (through objects, through philosophy), and finally, storage in a special spot—the cabinet.

In addition to princes and other royal collectors, artists (including Rembrandt, who was so interested in medicine) and doctors were also among the first to establish cabinets of curiosities. The close parallels between the cabinet of curiosities and surgery are clearly depicted in a 1610 engraving of the anatomical theater in Leiden. Objects explicitly designated as relics are gathered on the wooden balustrades reserved for spectators: animal skeletons and taxidermied birds, grouped in concentric circles mimicking circular models of the cosmos. Flanked by flag-waving vanitas allegories ("*Mors ultima linea rerum*"), the visitors follow the action at the center of the hall: the vivisection of a human, the apex of creation. Hunting trophies hang from the walls and an open cabinet at the back displays the tools of surgery, natural sciences (a telescope), and mathematics (a compass)—equipment that also played an elemental role in Bentham's philosophy. The dichotomy between knowledge and religion established in the Bible is addressed in this Baroque engraving. In the foreground of the picture, two skeletons stand on the balustrade and face an apple tree growing between them, a snake in its branches: a reenactment of the Fall. The formulation of the scientific validity claim that defined Bentham and Smith's experiment remains far in the distance.[32] The spiritual-moral framework and media repertoire of the theatrically staged cadaver, however, is fully developed. All of these aspects feed into the Auto-Icon.

VERA ANATOMIÆ LUGDUNO-BATAVÆ CUM SCELE₁IS ET RELIQVIS QVÆ IBI EXTANT DELINEATIO.

Anatomical theater at the University of Leiden, 1610.
Willem van Swanenburgh's engraving was based on a
drawing by Jan Cornelisz van't Woud (Woudanus).

The taxidermied philosopher is thus less an eccentric curiosity than he is the consistent continuation of occidental notions of the universe. Bentham's Auto-Icon compromises the very idea of the cabinet of curiosities, as it were. It transcends the dimensions of (pre-)museum collecting politics that had been established at that time and fuses elements of its visual practices in a single object. The automaton, skeleton, taxidermied animal, trophies, exotic finds (Bentham's nod to the Māori), and so forth: *Artificialia*, *Naturalia*, and *Exotica* are united in the Auto-Icon. And the idea of the ancestral portrait gallery is *incorporated* in the truest sense of the word. The consolidation into a singular exhibit-of-all comprised the moral meaning inherent in cabinets of curiosities (and museums). The systematizing, cataloging, explanation, and control of the world as a whole—allegorically identical to Bentham's panoptical-pannomionic-philosophical intentions—achieves figurative closure. In this way, the fusion between the body and teachings accomplished in Bentham's postmortem dissection is preserved forever. At the same time, it is elevated to a new level of meaning: the creation of the Auto-Icon turned the philosopher into his own world model.

The Auto-Icon, however, is not without further precursors. In Westminster Abbey, court chapel of the British crown, so-called funeral effigies constitute an almost uninterrupted parade of heirs apparent from the sixteenth to eighteenth centuries, starting with Henry VII.[33] The power ascribed to the wax figures—that is, sovereign power *in effigie*—as well as the context of their use changed over time, leaving many holes in the research to this day. One aspect that goes undisputed, though, is the motivation behind creating the figures. It serves as a direct continuation of the medieval conception of the king's two bodies—the material and symbolic bodies containing the ruler's god-given majesty.[34]

When the symbolic body loses its material counterpart in death, a conceptual void remains. It lasts from the death of a ruler until the coronation of the successor. To maintain a connection for the symbolic body in the interim, wooden (and later wax) dummies were invented to represent the deceased monarch as a living (!) person. The effigy, clothed in regalia and often moveable, headed the provisional government until the figure was transported—usually in triumphant posture atop the coffin—with the king's mortal remains to the funeral ceremony, whereupon it was installed either at or on the tomb in the church. This archaic ritual, which was practiced in France and Venice in addition to England, was upheld nearly until Bentham's time. And although the symbolic-political implications shifted in the seventeenth and eighteenth centuries (leading up to baroque conceptions of *memento mori*, for instance), the principal aspect remained potent: the expression, in act and effigy, of the king's inviolable and divinely ordained right to the throne.

Effigies were also widely used outside the monarchic-sacral symbolic field. In many world cultures, figures of kings and clerics are incinerated and desecrated in a recognized form of representative tyrannicide. The symbolic-political diminishment of effigies in the Baroque era—the transformation from replacement body to memorial object—required their reframing as de-emotionalized museum pieces. The effigy became an object of entertainment. From 1777 in France and 1802 in England, the trained physician Philippe Curtius and his protégée, the Alsatian wax sculptor Anna Maria Grosholtz (later known as Madame Tussaud), displayed likenesses of prominent political and cultural figures in their *salons de cire*; the statues were exhibited alongside images of anatomical monstrosities, whose designation as a "panopticon" ("curio collection") supplanted Bentham's neologism.[35] The fact that, despite its functional transformation, the visual form of the effigy did not vanish—but was instead absorbed by memorials of stone and metal—could be attributed to the "lifelike" impression made by wax, which appealed to a large audience.

In a direct parallel to the development of the panorama, the viewers' curiosity at Madame Tussaud's shifted from moralistic examples to causerie and the fun of "as if ..." games of conjecture, or optical illusions such as trompe l'œil. At the same time, this success forced the decoupling of dummy, monarchy, and cult. In 1775, the figure of William Pitts the Elder was the first effigy of a politician created as a public image outside the context of a funeral. Westminster

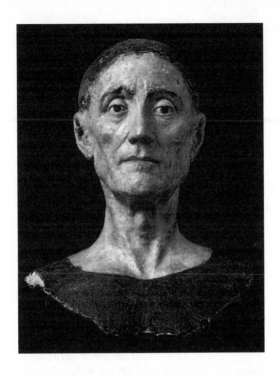

Wooden funeral effigy of King Henry VII. Westminster
Abbey, London, ca. 1509.

Abbey's very last wax figure, stripped of ritual and introduced as an attraction in 1805, was the likeness of national
hero Horatio Nelson, the fallen victor of Trafalgar, the man
who vanquished Napoleon. In the embattled waxworks
market, the figure contended against Madame Tussaud's
Nelson effigy as well as Nelson's actual funeral effigy, which
was on display in Saint Paul's Cathedral, where he was

buried. Within barely a century, the context surrounding wax figures had shifted permanently. Around 1720, while Margravine Sibylla Augusta did penance in the hermitage on the grounds of Schloss Favorite (Rastatt), encircled by "effigies" of the Holy Family, Philippe Curtius was staging the formal dinners of the king and his entourage in prerevolutionary France: visitors were allowed to touch the figures and their clothing and debate courtly fashions at length.[36] The visual form once associated with ceremony and religion had become common entertainment, an entrance-fee industry.

Although it would have been an obvious jab for Bentham the antimonarchist to make, an interpretation of the Auto-Icon as satirizing royal effigies and the divine right of kings comes up short. Regardless of whether these figures' original symbolic-political contextual range could still be decoded in Bentham's day, it had begun to blend so thoroughly with contemporary popular culture that the difference between historical church treasures and popular wax figure collections became impossible to discern. Furthermore, in the seventeenth century, loads of effigies in poor condition were cleared into a side wing of Westminster Abbey, where this "ragged regiment" further decayed and served as an attraction for tourists and the boys of Westminster School, where Bentham had started his own schooling in 1755 at age seven. The unheeding treatment of these supposed curiosities in the nave had an increasingly negative effect on the image of other, well-protected royal effigies. "Oh dear! you should not have such rubbish in the Abbey," an outraged visitor is said to have cried in the late 1800s.[37] Bentham

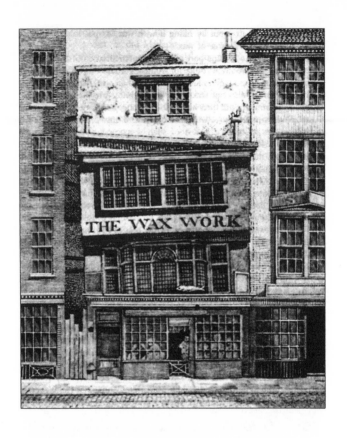

Mrs. Salmon's "Wax Work," in a lopsided house on Fleet Street, London. Engraving from 1793.

THE AUTO-ICON

responded in similar fashion when he tried to trump such vain frippery as "the lions, the wax-work, or the tomb" with moral edification in the inspection house, or when he connected every form of art with war, alcoholism, compulsive gambling, and an upper class incapable of reform, thereby denying it meaning. Bentham wanted his Auto-Icon to effect a media change in perspective when he promised: "The wax-works in the vaults of Westminster Abbey—Mrs Salmon's Museum in Fleet Street—yea, even Solomon in all his glory at the puppet-show, would dissolve before it."[38]

We can thus read Bentham's Auto-Icon as a critique of certain phenomena of a time that had chosen the road

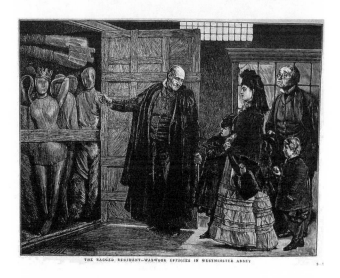

THE RAGGED REGIMENT—WAXWORK EFFIGIES IN WESTMINSTER ABBEY

Visitors at a presentation of discarded effigies from Westminster Abbey, the so-called ragged regiment. Engraving, post-1850.

Westminster Abbey, 1896

Wax effigy of King Charles II

Cabinet of effigies, with the wax figure of King Charles II (d. 1685) at the front. Photograph of the interior of Westminster Abbey, London, 1896.

toward mass culture. Wax figures and panoramas, cockfights and balloon flights, funeral processions and circuses, weekends at Ranelagh[39]—such forms of folk entertainment expressed a popularization that permeated all media and then reflected back onto reality. With the invention of lithography, high-circulation printed matter was made available to the public for the first time. The rise of the newspaper began. Starting in England, caricature as a new form of political criticism swept Europe. This changed propaganda, because despite regimented censorship, the media monopolies held by rulers were gradually softening. Napoleon was consistent in his response, in that he allowed for greater production of images.[40] Antonio Canova's bust in Possagno (1802), for instance, which depicts Napoleon as First Consul, was already dotted with green measuring points for manufacturing copies. With the spread of the empire, portraits of the sovereign were needed en masse, for display in the offices of occupied territories across the continent, where a new generation of civil servants bound by the *Code Napoléon* dominated the administration. The perennial war between image and counterimage was thus declared: a media spiral that successively reduces the viewer's sensibility and continuously expands their distance from ur-image and reality.

The Auto-Icon defied this development with a clear objective: an object that by definition is neither a portrayal, nor copy, nor media replacement, but nothing other than "a man who is his own image." "Auto-iconizing" is thus tantamount to the expulsion of the medium from the process of image creation. It is the separation of the image from its communication platform: the installation of the unmirrored, single valid reality as a picture of itself. In this way, Bentham's implied guiding theme of the "Vera-Icon" is advanced, which he defines as a reduplicated religious cult object based on the ur-image, itself not a human creation: an über-image that renounces media and artistic mediation and ascribes authenticity to its image, which is perceived

The Rotunda at Ranelagh Gardens. The pavilion, which
paralleled Bentham's Panopticon in form, enabled visitors
to stroll while listening to music. Interior painted by
Antonio Canaletto, 1754.

as "pictorial" and proven by means of thaumaturgy. The
Auto-Icon promotes this notion. As a sculpture built of the
body parts of the person depicted, the Auto-Icon circum-
vents the necessary process of reduplication in painting and
also does away with the model. It is its own ur-image, the
only possible original: authenticity in perfection. By means
of this process of media emancipation and purification, it
makes restitution for the aura that is lost in mass production. The allegorical significance of the "emblem" regains its
old power. In this way—and only this way—can the moral
example exercise influence on the observer.

REAL DUMMIES

The choice of the New Zealand iconizing process underscores Bentham's culturally critical intentions. The desired
return to the bare essentials was evidently only possible beyond the confines of Western cultural practice—it
required the "ingenuity" of the "noble savage." On the one
hand, this conceals Bentham's antipathy toward colonialism, the one-sided modus operandi of which was provoc-
atively reversed by the use of *mokomokai* on a member
of the colonial power. On the other hand, it also contains
a general anticivilization sentiment, echoes of which could
be found in the Romantic era, starting with Jean-Jacques
Rousseau. The triumph over cultural blindness through
edification: the template for societal reform outlined in the
"Inspection-House" gains an additional facet through the
Auto-Icon. At the same time, the political, religious, and cultural aberrations of civilization appear coequal in Bentham's
estimation. In their own ways, each is commented on and
contradicted, and not simply caught but overtaken—and
thus overcome. The Auto-Icon further exhausts the provo-
cation of the church introduced by vivisection. By pushing
the cult of icon and relic worship too far, Bentham exposes
it as a "false" media spectacle. He also repeatedly settled up
with the waxworks. While the London-based wax sculptor
Mrs. Mill (and later Madame Tussaud) advertised that everyone "may have their Effigies made of their deceas'd Friends,
on moderate Terms"[41]—to live with them at home!—the
first figure Madame Tussaud crafted herself, in 1777, was

of a famous philosopher, Voltaire. She exhibited him and the figure of Rousseau in many of her *salons de cire*, including in London. But a "real" philosopher, who vouched for his own teachings as an image of himself, no longer existed— neither in curio cabinet nor private collection.

Royal funeral effigies, wax figures, icons, relics, caricatures, portraits, commemorative engravings, early forms of photography, mass entertainment: the Auto-Icon is Bentham's sweeping media-political blow, his triumph of authenticity as an allegory of utilitarian veracity. Placed in the context of art, it also appears to be an entry in the debate with anatomy, which extended back to the Renaissance and was closely linked to discussions surrounding the formal poles of realism and stylization. This, then, returns us one more time to the field of medicine.

The study of dead bodies has led to hyperrealistic eruptions time and again, tied to everything from drastic affect to shock. Hans Holbein the Younger's predella (1521) in Basel, for instance, which depicts the Redeemer's decaying body, sparked prolonged debates about the boundaries of morality and permissible manners of representation; the picture was long concealed behind a curtain.[42] Rembrandt revealed his predilection for medicine in paintings such as *The Anatomy Lesson of Dr. Nicolaes Tulp* (1632, The Hague, Mauritshuis), a combination of group portrait and depiction of the vivisection of a cadaver. In the seven-by-five-meter oil painting *The Raft of Medusa* (1818, Paris, Louvre), Théodore Géricault attempted to give his work the suggestive power of an "authentic" ur-image and sketched body parts, including

To be seen in Exeter Change in the Strand,

as well in Christmas and other Holidays, and at all other Times, tho' the Change be shut, only then you must go in at that end towards Charing Cross.

Just
finish'd,
and to be
seen. The present
COURT of ENGLAND,
in Wax, after (and as
big as) the Life, in the
Inner-Walk of Exeter Change
in the Strand, much exceeding, tho'
both made by the most deservedly famous
Mrs. MILLS, whom in that Art all ingenious
Persons own had never yet an equal. The Names
of the Chief Persons, are the Queen, his Royal
Highness Prince George, the Princess Sophia, his Grace
the Duke of Marlborough, the Countess of Manchester,
the Countess of Kingston, the Countess of Musgrave, &c.
As likewise the Effigies of Mark Anthony, naturally
acting that which rendered him remarkable to the
World: Cleopatra, his Queen; one of her
Egyptian Ladies. Oliver Cromwell in
Armour: the Count Tollemach: with ma-
ny others too tedious here to mention. To be seen from 9 in the
Morn, till 9 at Night. You
may go in at any of the
Doors in the Change,
and pass thro' the
Hatter's Shop in
the Outward
Walks.

Note.—The Prices are Six Pence—Four Pence, and Two Pence a-Piece.

There is the Effigies of a Cornelian, walking behind the Queen.

☞ Persons may have their Effigies made of their deceas'd Friends, on moderate Terms.

Handbill from Mrs. Mill's Wax Work advertising the option to have one's deceased friends modeled in wax. London, late eighteenth century.

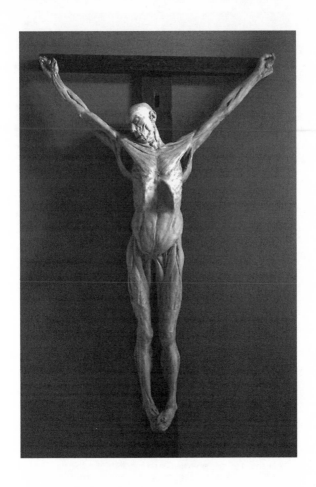

Thomas Banks and Joseph Constantine Carpue,
Anatomical Crucifixion, 1801. London, Royal Academy of
Arts.

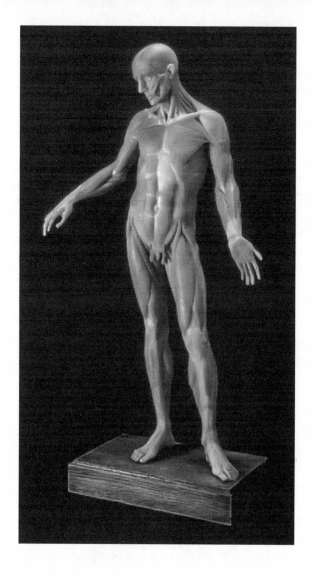

André-Pierre Pinson, *Ecorché humain* (Skinned human).
Anatomical wax model. Paris, ca. 1780.

the guillotined heads of convicts, in preparation.[43] The radical high point in the search for a scientifically founded realism in art was the joint attempt by painters Benjamin West and Richard Cosway, sculptor Thomas Banks, and surgeon Joseph Constantine Carpue. In October 1801, they nailed the body of the freshly executed murderer James Legg to a cross. The *Anatomical Crucifixion* was meant to help revise the supposedly common incorrect depiction of a body's deformation upon execution.[44] Carpue dissected and skinned the corpse in order to expose its muscles and tendons. Banks undertook a detailed plaster casting. It has been in the possession of the London Royal Academy of Arts since 1802, where it is shown to this day—not as a religious artwork, but as an object of study within the institute's collections.

This brutal experiment came about suddenly, without regard to either art or medicine. Even the anatomical wax models of the eighteenth century—which were manufactured as visual aids for students and acquired by enlightened monarchs such as Joseph II for the expansion of universities—were often posed in "lifelike" fashion. Sitting men, sans skin, flexed their muscles. Female bodies in erotic poses turned their innermost parts out on hinges. A London-based exhibit of anatomical wax figures in the 1770s showed preserved, real body parts alongside the dissected effigy of a very pregnant woman: fake blood flowed through glass veins, a pump moved the heart and lungs.[45] In the trompe l'œil of these artifacts, which circulated in surgeries and art academies alike, the final vestiges of cabinets

THE
ANALYSIS
OF
BEAUTY.

Written with a view of fixing the fluctuating IDEAS of
TASTE.

BY *WILLIAM HOGARTH.*

So vary'd he, and of his tortuous train
Curl'd many a wanton wreath, in sight of Eve,
To lure her eye.-------- Milton.

VARIETY

LONDON:

Printed by *J. REEVES* for the *AUTHOR,*
And Sold by him at his House in LEICESTER-FIELDS.

MDCCLIII.

William Hogarth, *The Analysis of Beauty*. Frontispiece
featuring a drawing of a "serpentine line" in a prism.
London, 1753.

of curiosities and the vanitas allegory kept cropping up—the pedagogical notion that had shifted its focus from morality to science. The reciprocal relationship between art and medicine here led the *Anatomical Crucifixion* to a final high point before its predecessors were absorbed by the entertainment industry, where they were to find an afterlife in waxworks, horror novels, and "Body Worlds" exhibits, liberated from all moral and scientific claims.

The disregard for convention, the pragmatic will for knowledge, the realism pushed to the point of intolerability, the historical connection to cabinets of curiosities and anatomical theater, and finally, the educational purpose reveal the kinship between the *Anatomical Crucifixion* and the Auto-Icon. Beyond its critique of civilization and media, Bentham's idea thus gains a further dimension: it is part of the academic discourse on the relationship between art and nature, on the rise of technology and science as the dominant culture of Europe, on positivistic "objectification," and on measuring the world and humankind. The painter William Hogarth had already attempted something similar in 1753, when he "scientifically" deciphered the principles of beauty with his gently curved "line of beauty," a serpentine ideal form said to underlie all aesthetic graces.[46]

Yet again, the considerable discrepancy between idea and execution of the Auto-Icon becomes clear. The artwork of David d'Angers—which provided the model for "Bentham's" wax head—was based (and this may be a hyperbolic formulation) on false physiognomic teachings found dredging the murky waters of metaphysics. Hogarth and the *Anatomical Crucifixion* were exploring temporal phenomenology with scientific-technical experimental design. Bentham attempted nothing short of the same in his discipline—philosophy—with the felicific calculus. The Panopticon would have been his "academy": as a place for education and training, and as a laboratory for testing and proving his theories. Consistent and utilitarian. As for what applied to members of the Royal Academy, Bentham also took matters into his own hands by allowing himself to be transformed into the Auto-Icon.

COSMIC THEATER

John Stuart Mill, the devoted pupil, painted a comprehensive picture of Bentham's character. He remained "a boy to the last," nonjudgmental of others and unencumbered by "self-consciousness, that daemon of the men of genius of our time, from Wordsworth to Byron, from Goethe to Chateaubriand, and to which this age owes so much both of its cheerful and its mournful wisdom."[47] Mill presents us with an image of altruism personified in Bentham, whose mild-mannered good nature epitomizes the integrity of his own teachings. Friedrich Engels, by contrast, reached different conclusions in his 1844 comparison of Bentham's work to Max Stirner's *The Ego and His Own*: "The noble Stirner ... takes for his principle Bentham's egoism, except that in one respect it is carried through more logically ... in the sense that Stirner as an atheist sets the ego above God ... whereas Bentham still allows God to remain remote and nebulous above him; that Stirner, in short, is riding on German idealism ... whereas Bentham is simply an empiricist."[48] Egoist, altruist, idealist, empiricist, reformer, and "radical fool": by means of the Auto-Icon, Bentham adds his own voice to the controversy surrounding his own figure and teachings. "Every man is his best biographer," the philosopher declared and revealed his very essence in the über-ur-image: a three-dimensional "auto-thanatography" with a claim to objectivity.

And how does Bentham introduce himself to us in his tangible autobiography? Above all else as a sociable fellow.

Beyond enjoying dinners with friends and chairing various utilitarian clubs, he also hoped for new companions for his Auto-Icon. Other, many, *all* people should give their bodies to science for the pleasure and edification of the living. All should allow themselves to be auto-iconized. Ancestral halls and city boulevards could be adorned with Auto-Icons. Authentic historical buildings could be constructed around them. A "temple of honour" for august figures and a "temple of dishonour" for traitors (Bentham suggested William Pitt the Younger and King George III) could be furnished with Auto-Icons. As examples of the good as well as the bad, a system illustrating punishment and reward, analogous to the Panopticon's grandiose stage play of "As If ...": "How instructive would be the vibrations of Auto-Icons between the two temples! The objects of the admiration of one generation might become objects of detestation to another." Bentham's "auto-iconic" cosmos is also an allegory of human yearning, a lesson from the principle of utility meant to uplift the human with regard to societal reform. Death— the driving force behind symbolic undoing and the master of socialistic dimensions—would thereby lose its frightful power. It would even make sense, what with the poor and rich enjoying the same chance at auto-iconic representation: "they would indeed 'meet together'—they would be placed on the same level." The world of the Auto-Icons would feature on earth that which religious projections of paradise had earmarked for the hereafter.

The Potemkin game of truth and perception is not exhausted in the theater of representation, however, for in utilitarianism, added moral value becomes measurable happiness only through material gain: much like educational progress in the Panopticon, the Auto-Icon's "reason" is directly equated with economic factors. For instance, Bentham enumerates the spending saved on gravesites, gravestones, and burial taxes. Auto-Icons would also be attractive for the open market. As with the trade in relics and *mokomokai* heads, the Auto-Icon business would exemplify the laws of the liberal market economy (provided it remain unobstructed by troublesome political regulations). The ethics and historical awareness of the living would directly decide supply and demand, because viewing an auto-iconized personage directly influences consumer interest. Depending on various factors, any given Auto-Icon might be worth two, three, or even several others. And taken as a whole, this difference ultimately enables a concrete calculation of the dominant societal morality.

Since money and happiness are so closely bound in the realm of the Auto-Icon—as in Bentham's vision of economic reality—the question of power also presents itself here. Bentham answers this question in the grand conclusion of his text on the Auto-Icon, in which he invites auto-iconized individuals from world history to join the cosmic theater. Bands and wires will puppeteer the made-up figures. Their voices will be imitated, their bodies made to "breathe" by unseen mechanisms: illusion and indistinguishability from reality are needed to dazzle the fickle audience intended to view this stage play—the same audience meant to visit the

Panopticon. Bentham designated "Bentham" the master of ceremonies. "He" enters the stage to introduce the *dramatis personae*. "He" seeks learned discussion on morality, ethics, justice, the state, law, logic, architecture, grammar. "Socrates," "Aristotle," "Plato," "Cicero," "Saint Paul," "Helvétius," "Etienne Dumont," "Euclid," "Newton," "Laplace," "Francis Bacon," "John Locke," "Montesquieu," "d'Alembert," "Vitruvius," "Samuel Bentham," "some important Italian architect," "Napoleon Bonaparte": they all stand on stage, waiting to be questioned by "Bentham," the solicitous emcee, the choreographer of his own apotheosis. "Bentham"—"the sage of the 1830th year after the Christian era"—outlines for "Aristotle" the advancements of the philosophy of happiness at the birth of a better world. "Bentham" pays homage to "Bacon," gardener of the "encyclopedic tree," where world knowledge and reason dovetail for the benefit of humankind. "Bentham" introduces "Bacon" to his correspondent "d'Alembert," the cultivator of this plant, whose golden fruits—"as if reared in the garden of the Hespirides"—Bentham had been privileged to harvest.

This major drama far surpasses the moral weight of the presentations in the Panopticon: "Bentham" delivers the triumphant message of human salvation through utilitarianism around the world. He does, however, require audience participation. At the end of the presentation, the viewers—gathered here on a "Quasi-hadji," a pilgrimage toward the greatest happiness principle—are to name the quasi-sacred Auto-Icon the winner as the most important Auto-Icon of all. They are to vote (like delegates of a united party at a congress where one can picture the reanimated Auto-Icons of Lenin and Mao in attendance) on "Bentham's" suggestion, which posits: of all the philosophers, wouldn't the actual savior have to be ... Bentham?

> Is not Bentham as good as Mahomet was? In this or that, however distant, age, will he not have done as much good as Mahomet will have done evil to mankind? But earlier than the last day of the earth, what will be the last day of the reign of the greatest-happiness principle? Here ends reverie—here ends the waking dream.[49]

Bentham's sense of mission was born of an era that venerated intellectuals, that looked to them to flood the earth with wisdom and the light of reason. Philosophers set trends; they were celebrated and courted like stars and exercised influence to the point of revolution. "Those two men have ruined France," Louis XVI said of Rousseau and Voltaire.[50] In life, Bentham was unable to meet the expectations built up by the luminaries. His Auto-Icon, however, is his triumphator. In the court of public opinion, it helps Bentham claim his self-declared right as the "legislator of the world." The lines between stage play and viewers dissolve: from London, the new Mecca, the Auto-Icon oversees the spread of a new world religion. It codifies a constitution that is valid the world over, thanks to universal human nature. "Bentham" thus establishes a new order on the basis of eternal laws: "Nature has placed mankind under the governance of two sovereign masters, *pain* and *pleasure*. It is for them alone to point out what we ought to do, as well as to determine what we shall do." In this new realm, established around the primacy of economics, a certain force is finally elevated to its rightful spot, a force that seeks—and, according to doctrine, creates—goodness. Because everyone is in search of happiness. And it is complemented by something that magically increases happiness: money.

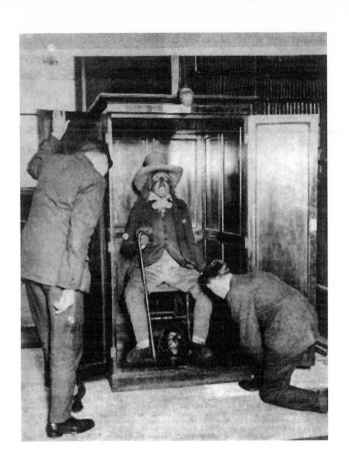

Appraisal of Jeremy Bentham's Auto-Icon, ca. 1950.

PRACTICE AFTER THEORY

Our audience with Jeremy Bentham is drawing to a close. His Panopticon has been construed as a symbol and an example of architecture, as a call for revolution and an instigator of prison reform, as an educational model and a world model, as an economic model and a state model, as a sacred building and an institute for researching and stimulating the human soul. The Auto-Icon has been interpreted as a critique of media and contemporary culture, as an über-ur-image to reinstate aura and allegory, then again as a model of the world and utilitarianism, as an academic contribution and philosophical last will and testament, as an act against church, state, colonialism, and grave robbery, as a deed for medical research, for the triumph of science and enlightenment to the benefit of humankind, as a tangible autobiography, as the founding document of a profane religion. But what does Bentham contribute to the visual manifestation of philosophy, politics, economics, and society in a greater, perhaps more current sense?

First, a word to those who may find the philosopher from London somewhat odd: they are in good company. Goethe called his contemporary a "radical fool," thus assigning him the single possible role a character like Bentham could hope to adopt in the age of the bourgeoisie. In the context of religion, the fool represented a skeptic who doubted the existence of God. In the context of the court, it was virtually his duty to criticize political and social conditions. Both aspects are reflected in Bentham's grand projects in applied philosophy, radicalized insofar as the fact that society in the age of Goethe had capped its attachment to religion and the court and thus had no more use for fools. The fools were now artists and philosophers. Goethe's solidarity with Bentham's intellectual passion could therefore be the result of an all-too-familiar feeling of exclusion.

Far less generous—and thus far more bourgeois, in their estimation—were those who thought little of "art" and called for a different form of political action than Bentham, namely Karl Marx and Friedrich Engels. Nowhere can more malicious commentaries on utilitarianism be found than in their writings. The severity of the contention had its root in the comparable aspirations of applied philosophy, because Marx/Engels and Bentham were competing purveyors of sociopolitical ideologies in the marketplace of practical reason, which had been hotly contested since Voltaire: the intellectual as the author of constitutions and legislation of real (and fictitious) states. To strengthen his own position in this game, Marx criticized his elder adversary Bentham, "that insipid, pedantic, leather-tongued oracle ... that could only have been manufactured in England." He exposes him as a "fool" who declines liberation from societal forces and instead philosophizes his way from a flawed to an unflawed life. Marx's fool does not stand outside the established order, he represents it: he is the bourgeoisie as a class-specific phenomenon, embodied *pars pro toto* by Bentham. "Had I the courage of my friend, Heinrich Heine, I should call Mr. Jeremy a genius in the way of bourgeois stupidity," Marx wrote in *Capital: Critique of Political Economy*.

The Liuthar Gospels (Aachen Cathedral Treasury), created around the year 1000, describe the coronation of Otto III by God's hand.

The cause of this stupidity lay in the central concept behind Bentham's applied philosophy. Marx deems fallacious the liberalism that was based in Adam Smith's teachings and formed the foundation for bourgeois self-legitimization:

> [The sphere of circulation or exchange of goods], within whose boundaries the sale and purchase of labour-power goes on, is in fact a very Eden of the innate rights of man. There alone rule Freedom, Equality, Property and Bentham. Freedom! because both buyer and seller of a commodity, say of labour-power, are constrained only by their own free will. They contract as free agents, and the agreement they come to, is but the form in which they give legal expression to their common will. Equality! because each enters into relation with the other, as with a simple owner of commodities, and they exchange equivalent for equivalent. Property! because each disposes only of what is his own. And Bentham! because each looks only to himself. The only force that brings them together and puts them in relation with each other, is the selfishness, the gain and the private interests of each. Each looks to himself only, and no one troubles himself about the rest, and just because they do so, do they all, in accordance with the pre-established harmony of things, or under the auspices of an all-shrewd providence, work together to their mutual advantage, for the common weal and in the interest of all.[1]

Bentham's ideas come across as a misunderstanding of those virtues cultivated in an age of revolution, virtues whose sole legitimate, consistent implementation in political practice would bear the name "Communism." Backward, then, was Bentham's assumption that all were equal before the law of the market. Backward, then, was his reducing *Homo sapiens* to *Homo oeconomicus*, whose actions were all in the service of accumulating capital and happiness. Backward, then, his belief that this would operate like clockwork, each component interacting in a self-regulating manner. Marx needs but a single paragraph to relegate Bentham to the sphere of circus charlatans, of magicians and their little tricks. Only those who believed in an "all-shrewd providence" could judge this otherwise—misunderstanding deceit as a "pre-established harmony of things" and recognizing the emergence of public interest from the sum of competing self-interests as a system constituted in a magical, even ghostly manner.

Marx's implicit allusion to this ghostliness points to the well-known *topos* of the "invisible hand," which, in the liberal notion of the market economy, is believed to turn self-interest into collective interest. Adam Smith invented the idea, more or less as a rhetorical lubricant for the central argument of his book, *The Wealth of Nations*:

> But the annual revenue of every society is always precisely equal to the exchangeable value of the whole annual produce of its industry. ... As every individual, therefore, endeavours as much as he can both to employ his capital in the support of domestic industry, and so to direct that industry that its produce may be of the greatest value; every individual necessarily labours

to render the annual revenue of the society as great as he can. He generally, indeed, neither intends to promote the public interest, nor knows how much he is promoting it. ... [And] by directing that industry in such a manner as its produce may be of the greatest value, he intends only his own gain, and he is in this, as in many other cases, led by an invisible hand to promote an end which was no part of his intention. ... By pursuing his own interest he frequently promotes that of the society more effectually than when he really intends to promote it.[2]

With the invisible hand, Smith places his readers in the position of a circus or theater audience beholding a magic show: they become believers, overcome by the desire to overpower. Economics as occultism, logic as magic, society as a mystical association. The invisible hand is that magical corrective that transforms chaos into order. In the occidental tradition, it represents a divine exercise of power that has been depicted in countless images: a hand extending from the clouds, often in an outstretched, judicial gesture—at times with a raised index finger—intervenes in the scene playing out below. In borrowing this metaphor, Smith implies a higher order, fixed far above humankind. This order operates in obscurity, but it represents a protective mechanism woven into the overall system. We are all "in God's hands."

This knowledge of a *force majeure*, which surpasses mere fate, inspires confidence and calm, even in the midst of hardship, deception, and dishonesty. In this way, and well before Bentham, Adam Smith framed the market economy as a religion, whose worship services took place not in the church but on the trading floor and in the banks. The "God" of the Newtonian era is honored here, a metaphor for the scientifically verifiable laws of nature. It is these laws that determine those of the market, logically fitted together by an invisible hand. The enduring success of an economic order whose advocates do not tire of rattling off praise of Adam Smith like a rosary could be due to this notion of a natural principle of economics.[3]

Although Smith never attempted to give the liberal ur-principle a practical (and at once symbolic) form, the magical essence of his teachings are immediately recognizable in Bentham's experimental design. The Panopticon and Auto-Icon are themselves works of magic. They are optical illusions of a possible totality that never reveals itself entirely, never divulges its rules. They are a concentration of affect; they are theater that beguiles the senses, causes the soul to founder, cuts the ground from under rationality. Like any good bit of sorcery, they are defined by spectral motives; indeed, the spectral is what holds them together at their core. The (in)visible overseer in the eye of the Panopticon, who guards the felicific calculus as one who sees apparitions, is specter and magician at once. The Auto-Icon, the living dead that Bentham believed should govern the earth with an invisible hand, is specter and magician at once. The charlatans of the eighteenth century appeared with similar trappings before their audiences of royalty and bourgeoisie clamoring for wealth and power; they vowed to turn iron ore into gold and build *perpetuum mobile* devices, and they peddled beauty and youth elixirs.[4] Given that at the same time, Adam Smith was depicting an invisible hand controlling the market economy and Bentham was positing a scientifically quantifiable happiness principle, the border between charlatan and "radical fool" can certainly be viewed as fluid.

It is in the very thrill of uncertainty, as to whether the wheels of the system are powered by deception or genius, that the irrepressible appeal of the invisible hand lies. It thus belongs to the class of the sublime. In his 1757 treatise *A Philosophical Enquiry into the Origin of Our Ideas of the Sublime and Beautiful*, the English philosopher and politician Edmund Burke provides a long list of strategies for overpowering people emotionally, influencing their feelings, and impairing their judgment. "Terror" makes the list, as do "Power," "Vastness," "Infinity," "Difficulty," and "Magnificence," but also "Light" and "Sound," "Pain" and "Pleasure"— all categories that found their way into Bentham's experimental design. A category to classify the invisible hand also makes Burke's list: "Obscurity." Every human senses its dark influence

> who considers how greatly night adds to our dread, in all cases of danger, and how much the notions of ghosts and goblins, of which none can form clear ideas, affect minds which give credit to the popular tales concerning such sorts of beings. Those despotic governments which are founded on the passions of men, and principally upon the passion of fear, keep their chief as much as may be from the public eye. The policy has been the

same in many cases of religion. Almost all the heathen temples were dark. Even in the barbarous temples of the Americans at this day, they keep their idol in a dark part of the hut, which is consecrated to his worship. For this purpose too the Druids performed all their ceremonies in the bosom of the darkest woods, and in the shade of the oldest and most spreading oaks.[5]

Burke creates a more plastic model for "Obscurity" by juxtaposing it with the enlightened or bright "Clearness." The more concrete the illustration or description of a thing, the less penetrating its emotional power of suggestion on the viewer or listener. The more obscure, the more sublime the depiction and thus the more profound the impact on the senses.

Burke's categories of the sublime not only hold a further key for the success of a system governed by the invisible hand, but also contain the root cause of Bentham's failure. The Panopticon and Auto-Icon transferred Adam Smith's obscure philosophy into clear scenarios, as Bentham employed examples to prove the utility of his teachings. He thereby stripped them of their magic. The concrete object—the Millbank prison blueprint, the taxidermied philosopher's corpse—produced a target that could infect the opinions of all those who had been sentenced to sublime silence by the invisible hand. The concrete object unequivocally revealed the failure of theory in practice.

Bentham seemed to fear nothing less when he decided to take the reins into his own hands to implement his world vision, to climb into the eye of the Panopticon, to allow

Stateville Prison, Illinois. Built 1919–1924. Historic postcard.

Presidio Modelo, a prison complex in Cuba built during the presidential dictatorship, 1926–1928.

PRACTICE AFTER THEORY

himself to be turned into an Auto-Icon. He thus tragically reveals how disquieted the enlightener feels at the Enlightenment, how frightened by the momentum an invention may gain, once set in the world, that in the worst case may deter imitators and cause misunderstanding. This double fate ultimately befell Bentham's experimental design. Rather than aid in prison reform, the Panopticon prisons of the nineteenth and twentieth centuries celebrated the most brutal forms of surveillance and punishment, solitary confinement, and oppression.[6] Rather than serve as the ur-image of an economic world order, the likeness of the capitalistic king of kings, the Auto-Icon was reduced to a laughable curiosity. Conversely, liberalism can be relieved that it was only peripherally associated with Bentham's final radical folly, which could have brought about its total miscarriage. Opponents of globalization have long made pilgrimages to London to see the idea of the free market economy decay *in effigie*. They would see the face of lucre in Bentham's disfigured head, the *Vera Icon* of capitalism, the perverted physiognomy of a person whose soul hustles on the streets of economics. It now reposes, thankfully, in a wooden box, locked away like the portrait of Dorian Gray, safeguarded in a refrigerated room, undying under ideal conditions—perhaps for all eternity—edged out of the focus of attention, marginalized to a foolish footnote in the inexorable victory parade of an economic order that most refer to simply as capitalism.

If Bentham's emblems of economic, political, and human progress were thus failures, the question arises as to whether the system of the invisible hand generated any of *its* own emblems. Based on biblical deadly sins, "greedy" capitalism produced plenty of negative imagery. Already by the sixteenth century, the triumvirate of usury, tyranny, and hypocrisy is depicted riding a "poor wicked donkey" (the people) against "Reason," "Justice," and the "Word of God."[7] In 1884, Walter Crane drew *The Capitalist Vampire*.[8] Carl Barks created the miser Scrooge McDuck, who swims through the money stored in his three-cubic-acre Money Bin.[9] But happiness, goodness, and humanity—which Smith and Bentham considered essential virtues of the market economy—did not inspire positive artistic allegories. While "electricity," "progress," "freedom," and "democracy" metamorphosed into female personifications over the course of the nineteenth century, "capitalism"—which of course enabled electricity, progress, freedom, and democracy in the first place—remained imageless.

Peter Flötner and Hans Sachs, "Tyranny, usury, and hypocrisy battle with the Word of God." Woodcut (handbill), 1525. Detail.

PRACTICE AFTER THEORY

"Democracy has no monuments. It strikes no medals. It bears the head of no man on a coin. Its very essence is iconoclastic."[10] John Quincy Adams, the sixth president of the United States, confessed this fear to his diary in 1831, out of anger over the Washington Monument, which had yet to be built in the capital. "Democracy" here refers to the specific self-perception of a nation founded on the premises of liberalism, a free market economy, and capitalism. Backed by gentleman farmers and slave owners like George Washington, the United States arose as an alliance to assert economic interests in defiance of British colonial rule, the young nation characterized by a pragmatic understanding of the state: politics provides the prerequisites for a flourishing economy. With the American Dream, which promises every honest worker wealth, happiness, and power, the United States raised the invisible hand to its original mythos, symbolically elevated by the "eye of God" and motto "*E pluribus unum*" in the national coat of arms. The amalgam of politics and economy (particularly evident in the form of presidential campaign finance) created a theocracy of capital that made "freedom" and "democracy" synonymous with "free trade" and "market economy" (these synonyms find their rhetorical uses when, for instance, oil and weapons deals with dictators are deemed expressions of "change through trade" and the export of "Western values").

Land of the free, legacy of antiquity, embodiment of Enlightenment ideals, champion of modern democracy, gold standard of the world: in each of these scenarios, whose power lies in noble simplicity, the actual engine of

Walter Crane, *Capitalist Vampire*, 1884. To the right, the
personification of socialism.

PRACTICE AFTER THEORY

political action remains invisible. The state is the vehicle for pushing financial-political interests and satisfying human emotion, while capital (with its intrinsic promise of plea-sure) on its own is apparently unable to achieve the same result of satisfaction. The "state" translates "economics" into visual form, insofar as parliaments and councils stage the drama of power and happiness, human will and super-human providence, following a script drafted by an invisible hand. It always then becomes reality the moment the econ-omy turns to the state in order to stabilize the system.[11]

This (schematically presented) reciprocity is exempli-fied by Washington, DC, which evolved from 1792 onward as an ideal setting for a democratic residence. It unifies the aspects of city planning, architecture, art, ceremony, and memorial in a monumental tapestry of meaning, as it were woven together in the Capitol—the heart of city and state. What is not immediately evident is the extent to which the emergence of this structure was tied to the economy: every crisis yielded the next boom in construction, the sum of these crises resulting in the grandeur of the metropolis.[12] Even during the Civil War (1861–1865), work commenced to complete the Washington Monument and expand Capitol Hill. The recession from 1907 to 1910 and the New Deal, which followed the worldwide economic crash of 1929, led to extensive work on the seat of government, based on his-torical plans from 1792. These expansions reached their pinnacle in 1941 with the new construction of the Pentagon, new home of the Defense Department (then the Department of War) and the world's largest office building. Further

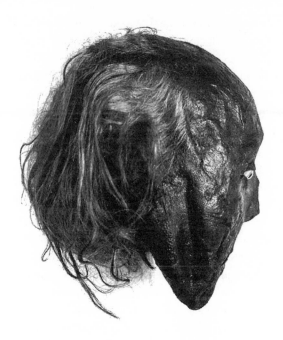

Jeremy Bentham's head, side and frontal views.
Photographs from the journal *Biometrika* (1904) on the
occasion of a physiognomic evaluation.

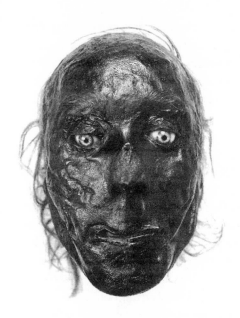

measures to expand Washington came in the final years of the Vietnam War, with new additions to the Library of Congress and National Gallery of Art.[13] Since 2001, the city has been reshaped with surveillance and security infrastructure. Touting the term "green building," the current construction work draws the notion of so-called sustainability into the equation.

Washington, with its buildings and its bureaucrats, can be seen as one big economic stimulus package, at once both real and symbolic and—in its cliché ideality—the model for many other states in the world. In all of these states, the political iconography appears as a photographic negative, as it were, of a capitalistic iconography, which does not exist on its own terms. All that is visible are parallel phenomena created by capitalism, which conjures them up from the state like rabbits pulled from a hat. The greatest of these state tricks, rivaled only by Jesus changing water into wine, occurred toward the end of the eighteenth century, an era rife with tricks: a thin layer of color applied on the paper currency magically turns the bill into a relic, whose god-given significance, as it were, is recognized by all. This experiment's unassailable power arises from the specific symbols depicted: the symbols of the state, whose presses print the currency. Stroke of genius, charlatanry, or both? In any case, nothing could be opposed to an idea this sublime— not even the most radical folly.

PRACTICE AFTER THEORY

NOTES

THE THEORY BEHIND THE PRACTICE

1. Jeremy Bentham, *Panopticon*, "Postscript I: Plan of Construction, Section VIII, Inspection-Galleries and Lodge" (London, 1791), 60. In an effort to collect and contain the flood of Bentham's texts, University College London created the website http://www.utilitarian.net/betham/index.htm. Two pieces temporarily available there were critical to the first part of this text: Simon Werret, "Potemkin and the Panopticon: Samuel Bentham and the Architecture of Absolutism in 18th Century Russia" (lecture manuscript, 1998) and Philip Steadman, "The Contradictions of Jeremy Bentham's Panopticon Penitentiary," *Journal of Bentham Studies* 9 (2007).

2. Walter Gropius, quoted in Ulrich Conrads, ed., *Programs and Manifestoes on 20th-Century Architecture* (Cambridge, MA: MIT Press, 1970), 46.

3. Jeremy Bentham, *Panopticon, or The Inspection-house* (London, 1791), 139–140. Bentham reprised the anthemic summary in the first postscript of the *Panopticon*.

4. The term "radical," coined in the eighteenth century and applied to a motley league of intellectual political reformers, gradually seeped into the description of political philosophy. See Elie Halévy's seminal work, *La formation du radicalisme philosophique* (Paris: Félix Alcan, Éditeur, 1904). See also Glenn Burgess and Matthew Festenstein's edited collection, *English Radicalism, 1550–1850* (Cambridge: Cambridge University Press, 2007), esp. 217–240 on Bentham.

5. See Jacques-Alain Miller, "Jeremy Bentham's Panoptic Device," *October* 41 (Summer 1987), and "Jeremy Bentham's

Panoptic Machinery," in Jacques-Alain Miller, Miran Božovič, and Renata Salecl, *Utilitarismus* (Vienna: Turia + Kant, 1996), 7–51. Originally published as "Le despotisme de l'Utile: La machine panoptique de Jeremy Bentham," *Ornicar? Bulletin periodique du Champ freudien* 3 (1975): 3–36. Pascal Kané's 1979 documentary bore the title "La machine panoptique."

6. Jeremy Bentham, *Panopticon*, "Postscript II: A Plan of Management, Section XIII" (London, 1791), 196. See also Marco E. L. Guidi, "'My Own Utopia': The Economics of Bentham's Panopticon," *European Journal of the History of Economic Thought* 11, no. 3 (2004): 405–431. See also Nathalie Sigot, *Bentham et l'économie: Une histoire de l'utilité* (Paris: Economica, 2001).

7. Jeremy Bentham, *Principles of Penal Law, Part III: Indirect Means of Preventing Crimes*, in *The Works of Jeremy Bentham* (Edinburgh: John Bowring, 1838–1843), vol. 1, part 2, 557: "If it were the custom to imprint the titles of the nobility upon their foreheads, these marks would become associated with the ideas of honour and power."

8. Jeremy Bentham, *Panoptique: Mémoire sur un nouveau principe pour construire des maisons d'inspection, et nommément des maisons de force*, ed. Etienne Dumont (Paris, 1791). The following publications study the extensive differences between the text versions: Cyprian Blamires, *The French Revolution and the Creation of Benthamism* (Houndmills: Palgrave Macmillan, 2008); Emmanuelle de Champs and Jean-Pierre Cléro, eds., *Bentham et la France: Fortunes et infortunes de l'utilitarisme* (Oxford: Voltaire Foundation, 2009). The latter text includes critical essays on Bentham's reception in the twentieth century. Bentham's vehement dispute with French politics is documented in Philip Schofield, Catherine Pease-Watkins, and Cyprian Blamires, eds., *Rights, Representation and Reform: Nonsense upon Stilts and Other Writings on the French Revolution* (Oxford: Oxford University Press, 2002). Regarding Bentham's reception in Germany,

see the editor's preface in Jeremy Bentham, *Grundsätze der Civil- und Criminal-gesetzgebung*, ed. Friedrich Eduard Beneke (Berlin: Etienne Dumont, 1830). On page iv, he writes: "Only in Germany has Bentham gone unknown and unused until recently."

9. See Janet Semple, *Bentham's Prison: A Study of the Panopticon Penitentiary* (Oxford: Oxford University Press, 1993), 2–13. Semple attributes Foucault's inadequate interpretation of Bentham to limited exposure and a lack of knowledge of the greater context. See also Anne Brunon-Ernst, "Foucault Revisited," *Journal of Bentham-Studies* 9 (2007). We must not forget the classic anticapitalistic critique of the bourgeoisie: Léon Bloy, *Exégèse des Lieux communs* (Paris: Mercure de France, 1902).

10. Even Janet Semple, who combats misinterpretations of the *Panopticon* for over three hundred pages, ultimately draws parallels to "Orwell's Big Brother, Tolkien's Dark Lord, or the hideous reality of the clattering surveillance towers along the old Berlin Wall." Semple, *Bentham's Prison*, 316. The shift in interpretation to one of psychological torture can be followed in Ruxandra Cesereanu, *Panopticon: Political Torture in the Twentieth Century: A Study of Mentalities* (Bucureşti: Institutul Cultural Român, 2006).

THE PANOPTICON

1. For a detailed look at the adventures of the Bentham brothers, see Ian R. Christie, *The Benthams in Russia, 1780–1791* (Oxford: Berg, 1993).

2. Sebag Montefiore, *Prince of Princes: The Life of Potemkin* (London: Macmillan, 2000); Jena Detlef, *Potemkin: Favorit und Marschall Katharinas der Großen* (Munich: Langen Müller, 2001).

3. See Martin Warnke, *Hofkünstler: Zur Vorgeschichte des modernen Künstlers*, 2nd ed. (Cologne: DuMont Buchverlag, 1986).

4. *The Works of Jeremy Bentham*, vol. 11, *Panopticon Corre-spondence* (Edinburgh: John Bowring, 1838–1843), 97. (Selections from *History of the War between Jeremy Bentham and George III, by One of the Belligerents*, published 1830–1831.)

5. During a second sojourn in Russia, Samuel built the Panopti-con School of Arts in Saint Petersburg in 1806. A very English adaptation of ancient Greco-Roman theater design was Shakespeare's Globe Theatre, another formal predecessor of the Panopticon. See Anna Radzun, "Zur Geschichte der Anat-omie und der anatomischen Theater," in *Palast des Wissens: Die Kunst- und Wunderkammer Zar Peters des Großen*, ed. Brigitte Buberl and Michael Dückershoff (Munich: Hirmer, 2003).

6. *The Works of Jeremy Bentham*, vol. 11, 97–98.

7. See Montefiore, *Prince of Princes*, 333–334, 341–343.

8. For Jeremy's activities in Crimea leading up to his departure from Russia, see Christie, *The Benthams in Russia*, 185–232, and Montefiore, *Prince of Princes*, 333–334, 341–343.

9. Bentham sent the letters to his father in London. In published form, the recipient is made anonymous, which heightens the letters' literary quality. Such philosophical pieces (and count-less other forms) were presented as fictionalized exchanges in response to the popular genre of epistolary novels. Cf. Rousseau's *La nouvelle Héloïse* (1761)—a philosopher's novel—and Schiller's *Über die ästhetische Erziehung des Menschen* (1793)—a novelist's philosophy. Even Bentham's *Defence of Usury* (London: Payne and Foss, 1787) was pre-sented as a series of letters.

10. Semple, *Bentham's Prison*, 14. A limited run of the first ver-sion of the *Panopticon* was published in London in 1786.

11. Charles François Philibert Masson, *Secret Memoirs of the Court of Petersburg* (London: 1800), 110; cited in Montefiore, *Prince of Princes*.

12. On November 25, 1791, Bentham alerted Jean-Philippe Garran-Coulon (who, as a member of the legislative committee of the Assemblée nationale, was responsible for reforming criminal justice) that he was sending him a copy of the *Panopticon*: "France is the country, above all others, in which any new idea—provided it be a useful one—is most readily forgiven." *The Works of Jeremy Bentham*, vol. 10 (Edinburgh: John Bowring, 1838–1843), 269.

13. Jeremy Bentham, *Panopticon*, "Postscript II: A Plan of Management, Section XIV, Punishments" (London, 1791), 201.

14. *The Works of Jeremy Bentham*, vol. 10, 156–157. Reveley, employed as an illustrator, accompanied the prominent English nobleman and politician, "Sir R. W." (Richard Worsley), on what seems to have been the latter's grand tour through Greece. During this time, the architect was studying the third volume of Stuart and Revett's *Antiquities of Athens* (1794; the travel manuscript is now housed in the archives of the Royal Institute of British Architects). Bentham and Reveley appear to have connected over a shared contempt for the nobleman. Bentham reports that Worsley later visited him in Krychaw. Bentham's memoirs do not indicate whether Reveley was present during this visit, during which he may have seen Samuel's Panopticon with his own eyes. More on Reveley (1760–1799) can be found in the *Oxford Dictionary of National Biography* (http://www.oxforddnb.com/) and *Biographical Dictionary of English Architects 1660–1840* (London: J. Murray, 1954). Reveley's propensity for unusual ideas can be seen in his 1796 proposals to straighten the River Thames in east London.

15. Alexander Taylor Milne, ed., *The Correspondence of Jeremy Bentham*, vol. 4, *October 1788 through December 1793* (London: Athlone Press, 1981), Letter 714, Bentham to John Parnell, August 30, 1790, 188.

16. Ibid., Letter 741, Bentham to John Parnell, February 1, 1791, 232.

17. See Bentham's explanatory missive to his publisher John Bowring, dated January 24, 1821, with an image of the engraving and the note: "The Plates referred to in this work [the *Panopticon*] were destroyed by a fire at the printer's. An improved plan of construction is shown in a small plate inserted in the work entitled 'Pauper Management improved.'" *The Works of Jeremy Bentham*, vol. 4 (Edinburgh: William Tait, 1838–1843; London: John Bowring, 1843), 171–172. See also Bentham's letter to King George III, dated May 11, 1791, ibid., vol. 9, 260–261. A detailed history of this edition can be found in *A Bibliographical Catalogue of the Works of Jeremy Bentham* (Tokyo: Chuo University Library, 1989), 108–118. See also Milne, *The Correspondence of Jeremy Bentham*, Letter 786, 300, in which Jan Ingenhousz confirms delivery of a copy of the "Panopticon containing three copper plates" on May 27, 1791. The plans for "Pauper Management Improved" (1812, inserted between pages 88 and 89 in the edition held by UCL) are labeled "Samuel Bentham, invenit, Samuel Bunce, delineavit," and differ in both the structure and the look and feel of Reveley's project. The originals of the various stages of planning are housed in the Bentham section of the Special Collections Department at UCL: 115/43, 115/44, 115/119a, 115/126, 118/174, 119a/124, 119a/127, 119a/119, 119a/122, 119a/127, 119a/129, 151/66a,b.

18. For an extensive discussion on the relationship between the poor law and the Panopticon, see Jeremy Bentham, *Writings on the Poor Law*, 2 vols. ed. Michael Quinn (Oxford: Oxford University Press, 2001, 2010). See also Anne Brunon-Ernst, *Le Panoptique des pauvres: Jeremy Bentham et la réforme de l'assistance en Angleterre (1795–1798)* (Paris: Presses de la Sorbonne Nouvelle, 2007).

19. "Panopticon versus New South Wales: Or, The Panopticon Penitentiary System, and the Penal Colonization System, Compared," in a letter addressed to the Right Honorable Lord Pelham (1802), in *The Works of Jeremy Bentham*, vol. 4.

London's Millbank Prison, which Bentham helped develop until 1813, served as the central hub for gathering all British prisoners being shipped to Australia; this practice did not end until 1868. A further version of the Panopticon can also be found in Jeremy Bentham, *Proposal for a New and Less Expensive Mode of Employing and Reforming Convicts* (London, 1798).

20. While there, he wrote a draft of his will, dated August 17, 1789. University College London, Special Collections Department, Bentham Collection 173/34b, The Will of Jeremy Bentham.

21. Bentham saw to it that this plan reached his many long-term correspondents, including Mirabeau, La Rochefoucauld, and Lafayette. See also a letter Samuel and Jeremy Bentham wrote to Lord St. Helens on July 8, 1791, in *The Works of Jeremy Bentham*, vol. 9, 261–262. At the same time, Bentham was attempting to disseminate his ideas on reforming constitutional law in France.

22. These so-called Bridewells, named after their place of origin (an abandoned castle), were in as neglected a state as the prisons. For a history of prisons, see Michael Ignatieff, *A Just Measure of Pain: The Penitentiary in the Industrial Revolution 1750–1850* (New York: Pantheon Books, 1978); Mitchel P. Roth, *Prisons and Prison Systems: A Global Encyclopaedia* (Westport, CT: Greenwood Press, 2006); Richard van Dülmen, *Theater des Schreckens: Gerichtspraxis und Strafrituale in der frühen Neuzeit*, 4th ed. (Munich: C. H. Beck, 1995); Pieter Spierenburg, *The Prison Experience: Disciplinary Institutions and Their Inmates in Early Modern Europe* (New Brunswick: Amsterdam University Press, 1991); Thomas Nutz, *Strafanstalt als Besserungsmaschine: Reformdiskurs und Gefängniswissenschaft 1775–1848* (Munich: De Gruyter Oldenbourg, 2001). On the development of corrections in England up to present day, see Yvonne Jewkes, ed., *Handbook on Prisons* (Cullompton: Routledge, 2007). See also Yvonne Jewkes and

Jamie Bennett, eds., *Dictionary of Prisons and Punishment* (Cullompton: Routledge, 2008) and Tim Newburn, ed., *Dictionary of Policing* (Cullompton: Routledge, 2008).

23. Jeremy Bentham, *A View of the Hard-Labour Bill; Being an Abstract of a Pamphlet, Intituled "Draught of a Bill, to Punish by Imprisonment and Hard Labour, Certain Offenders; and to Establish Proper Places for their Reception." Interspersed with Observations Relative to the Subject of the Above Draft in Particular, and to the Penal Jurisprudence in General* (London: T. Payne and Sons, 1778).

24. For more on this development, see Robin Evans, *The Fabrication of Virtue: English Prison Architecture 1750–1840* (Cambridge: Cambridge University Press, 1982). See also Norman B. Johnston, *Forms of Constraint: A History of Prison Architecture* (Urbana: University of Illinois Press, 2000) and Andreas Bienert, *Gefängnis als Bedeutungsträger: Ikonographische Studie zur Geschichte der Strafarchitektur* (Frankfurt: Peter Lang, 1996).

25. *Panopticon*, "Postscript I: Plan of Construction," para. IX, XXII, and XXIII, in *The Works of Jeremy Bentham*, vol. 87, 110–115.

26. See Bentham's extensive letters to Sir John Parnell, in Milne, *The Correspondence of Jeremy Bentham*, Letter 711, Bentham to Parnell, August 26–27, 1790, 171–179, and Letter 714, August 30, 1790, 185–192. See also the following letters, all regarding the Irish project, including correspondence to Reveley: Letter 738 to William Pitt, January 23, 1791, 223–229; Letter 749 to Landsdowne regarding Poland, 243–254; and Letters 786 and 791 regarding Haarlem, 300, 309.

27. Milne, *The Correspondence of Jeremy Bentham*, Letter 874 to Jean Marie Roland de la Platière, October 16, 1792, 401.

28. Ibid., Letter 792, 310–311. See also the letters to Reginald Pole Carew, who had established Bentham's contact with Adam, as well as the Letter 789 to Robert Adam, and Letter 848 to James Adam.

29. Adam's plans, which included an epigraph reminiscent of Bentham's panoptic flexibility ("To serve as gaol, Bedlam or Infirmary if whole is built"), are housed in the archives at Sir John Soane's Museum, Vol. 33, 9–34, with variations in Vols. 21, 12, and 224, Vol. 1, 74. On the drawing in the collection, see Walter L. Spiers, *Catalogue of the Drawings and Designs of Robert and James Adam in Sir John Soane's Museum* (Cambridge: Chadwyck-Healey, 1979). On the Adams, see David King, *The Complete Works of Robert and James Adam and Unbuilt Adam*, 2 vols. (Oxford: Routledge, 2001).

30. At the same time, Bentham received a two-thousand-pound advance of tax money for his work. See *The Works of Jeremy Bentham*, vol. 11, 167 ("Examination of Jeremy Bentham, Esquire, June 23, 1798").

31. Letter from Bentham to John Bowring on January 24, 1824, in *The Works of Jeremy Bentham*, vol. 4:

   The design of building a Panopticon prison lingered from 1791 to 1813, when, by the erection of another prison [Millbank], without any of the advantages, and more than ten times the expense, it was finally extinguished. ... After delays upon delays, an act of Parliament was passed, by which the faith of Parliament was pledged to the author for the adoption of his plan; and at last, in 1813, another act to authorise the violation of that pledge. To prepare for this violation, a Committee of the House of Commons had been got up by the Secretary of State, Lord Sidmouth. The plan had been recommended by the famous Finance Committee of 1797–8, of which Mr. Abbott, afterwards Speaker, now Lord Colchester, was chairman. A contract had been entered into, and in consequence the author put into possession of a spot of land. For the commencement of the business, the signature of George III was necessary; after an unexampled delay of three weeks, that signature was at length peremptorily refused. The official correspondence on the subject would fill a volume. To the all accessible and inspectable prison in question, Lord Sidmouth has substituted a Bastile, not to be visited, without his order, even by constituted authorities.

For more on the Millbank project, see Semple, *Bentham's Prison*. On Bentham's compensation, see *The Works of Jeremy Bentham*, vol. 11, 106.

32. For more background, see Mark E. Kann, *Punishment, Prisons and Patriarchy: Liberty and Power in the Early American Republic* (New York: NYU Press, 2005), and Eleanor Conlin Casella, *The Archeology of Institutional Confinement* (Gainesville: University Press of Florida, 2007).

33. "The king's rule over the land was nothing other than a disincorporation and reincorporation of the ruler's command over his home and court." Norbert Elias, *Die höfische Gesellschaft: Untersuchungen zur Soziologie des Königtums und der höfischen Aristokratie* (Frankfurt: Suhrkamp, 2002), 76. Elias's study (101ff in particular) provides important insight into the political-structural stratification of space in the court of Louis XIV, inside the royal residence, and beyond. On 110, he writes: "The differentiated curation of exteriors as an instrument of social differentiation—representing status through form—is not only characteristic of houses, but of the courtly way of life as a whole." Wolfgang Braunfels's classic work explores this formal development further: *Abendländische Stadtbaukunst: Herrschaftsform und Baugestalt* (Cologne: DuMont Reiseverlag, 1976). On central perspective, see Hubert Damisch, *The Origin of Perspective*, trans. John Goodman (Cambridge, MA: MIT Press, 1995).

34. Within the context of architectural theory, these figures are part of a two-hundred-year-old debate regarding the configuration of the ideal city. Formal parallels between centralized ideal cities and the Panopticon clearly exist. (See, e.g., plans drafted by/for Antonio Filarete, 1461; Girolamo de Maggi, 1564; Palma Nova, 1593; Jacques Perret, 1601; Daniel Speckle, 1608; Roland Levirloys, 1770.) For more on ideal

cities and absolutistic city planning, the works of Albert Erich Brinckmann are still worth consulting. A further formal parallel can be found in Isidore Canevale's Narrenturm in Vienna (1784). Its similarities are all in the exterior; the interior structure of this early psychiatric ward is utterly distinct.

35. Elias, *Die höfische Gesellschaft*, 76, n. 3. To what degree Ledoux's design is abstracted from the metaphor of the king as the sun (an image popular since Louis XIV) also warrants discussion. See Peter Burke, *The Fabrication of Ludwig XIV* (New Haven: Yale University Press, 1992). See also Hendrik Ziegler, *Der Sonnenkönig und seine Feinde: Die Bildpropaganda Ludwigs XIV in der Kritik* (Petersberg: Michael Imhof, 2010).

36. This design traces back to the inventive Mannerist styles of Palladianism.

37. This context would also include Antoine Watteau's or François Boucher's paintings, as well as the bucolic festival and dance music of the time. For more on Hameau and Versailles, see Christian Baulez, *Versailles: Deux siècles d'histoire de l'art: Etudes et chroniques* (Versailles: Société des Amis de Versailles, 2007), 233–234. More generally, see also Ruth und Dieter Groh, *Zur Kulturgeschichte der Natur*, 2 vols. (Frankfurt: Suhrkamp/Insel, 1996). For a concise depiction, see Jürgen von Stackelberg, *Jean-Jacques Rousseau: Der Weg zurück zur Natur* (Munich: W. Fink, 1999).

38. See also the analysis in Hanno-Walter Kruft, *Städte in Utopia: Die Idealstadt vom 15. bis zum 18. Jahrhundert zwischen Staatsutopie und Wirklichkeit* (Munich: C. H. Beck, 1989), 112–126. For a comprehensive study of Chaux, see Gérard Chouquer and Jean-Claude Daumas, eds., *Autour de Ledoux. Architecture, Ville et Utopie* (Besançon: PU de Franche-Comté, 2008). Claude-Nicholas Ledoux, who was imprisoned as a royalist during the revolution, reinterpreted Chaux after his release, placing it in the context of a democratic political order: "Architecture considérée sous le rapport de l'art, de

moeurs et de la legislation [Architecture considered in relation to art, customs, and legislation]" (Paris, 1804). A recasting of the absolutist apparatus of city planning with new democratic content can also be seen in the planning of Washington, DC.

39. Jeremy Bentham, *The Influence of Time and Place on Legislation*, in *The Works of Jeremy Bentham*, vol. 1, 194.

40. For more on the correlation of these motifs, see Gerhard Charles Rump, ed., *Gefängnis und Paradies: Momente in der Geschichte eines Motivs* (Bonn: Habelt, 1982). On perceptions of paradise in the eighteenth century, see Brigitte Peucker, *Arcadia to Elysium: Preromantic Modes in 18th Century Germany* (Bonn: Bouvier Verlag Herbert Grundmann, 1980).

41. Edmund Burke's gripping descriptions in *Reflections on the Revolution in France* (London: J. Dodsley, 1790) significantly influenced British reserve toward the French Revolution, which would be confirmed with France's declaration of war. The antipodal view of the different paths to freedom is illustrated in Thomas Rowlandson and George Murray's widely disseminated 1792 caricature "The Contrast."

42. Milne, *The Correspondence of Jeremy Bentham*, Letter 856, Bentham to Marquis Lansdowne, August 9, 1792, 380. On Bentham's relationship with France, see Philip Schofield, *Utility and Democracy: The Political Thought of Jeremy Bentham* (Oxford: Oxford University Press, 2006), esp. 78–108.

43. Julian Hoppit, *A Land of Liberty? England 1689–1727* (Oxford: Oxford University Press, 2000); George Norman Clarke, *The Reign of George III: 1760–1815* (Oxford: Oxford University Press, 1960); Asa Briggs, *England in the Age of Improvement 1783–1867* (London: Routledge, 1999). On the relationship between England and France, see Hans-Christof Kraus, *Englische Verfassung und politisches Denken im Ancien Régime 1689–1789* (Munich: De Gruyter Oldenbourg, 2006). Jane Austen's *Sense and Sensibility* (1811) also provides a fictionalized account of the Georgian era.

44. Günter Barudio, *Das Zeitalter des Absolutismus und der Aufklärung 1648–1779* (Frankfurt: Fischer Taschenbuch, 1981), 329.

45. City development, led by the father-son architect duo of John Wood the Elder and the Younger, accelerated post-1750. Iris Loosen-Frieling, *Architektur zwischen Norm und Geschmack: Die Platzarchitektur von John Wood dem Älteren und John Wood dem Jüngeren in Bath* (Hildesheim: Georg Olms, 1992); Michael Forsyth, *Bath* (New Haven, CT: Yale University Press, 2003). A catalog by Sheila O'Connell, Roy Porter, Celina Fox, and Ralph Hyde provides insight into London at that time: *London 1753* (Boston: David R. Godine, 2003).

46. *De l'Esprit des lois* (Geneva, 1748). Montesquieu developed his system on the basis of an absolutist division of power. Of the extensive literature on the subject, see esp. Alain Cambier, *Montesquieu et la liberté: Essai sur De l'esprit des lois* (Paris: Editions Hermann, 2010).

47. On Beckford (the Elder), see Richard B. Sheridan's comprehensive entry in the Oxford Dictionary of National Biography. See also Walter Besant, *London in the Eighteenth Century* (London: Adam & Charles Black, 1903), 23–27. Bentham mentions the event in "The Rationale of Punishment" (1830), ch. 3, Forfeiture of Reputation:

> He who blames the proceedings of a man in power, justly or unjustly, is a libeller: the more justly, the worse libeller. But for blaming the proceedings of men in power, and as they think justly, never will the people of this country look upon a man as infamous. Lawyers may harangue, juries may convict; but neither those juries, nor even those lawyers, will in their hearts look upon him as infamous. (Note: In 1758, Dr. Shebbeare, was pilloried for writing a libel against the then King, under a Whig administration. He stood in triumph: the people entertained him with applause. At another time, J. Williams, bookseller, was pilloried for publishing a libel against his Majesty George the Third, under

an administration charged with Toryism: the people made a collection for him. At another time, W. Beckford, Lord Mayor of London, replied extempore, in an unprecedented and affrontive manner, to a speech from the throne: the citizens put up his statue in Guildhall. Shame did not then, I think, follow the finger of the law.)

John Timbs's piece (*English Eccentrics and Eccentricities* [London: Richard Bentley, 1866], 22–23) points out that the inscription on the monument includes wording retroactively attributed to Beckford that was not part of his tirade against the king.

48. The statue was built from 1770 to 1772, following John Francis Moore's design; two years prior, Moore had crafted a Beckford monument, which can be viewed today at Ironmongers' Hall, Shaftesbury Place, London. For more on sculpture, see Philip Ward-Jackson, *Public Sculpture of the City of London* (Liverpool: Liverpool University Press, 2003), 163–166. Beckford's likeness was repeatedly moved in Guildhall, including to make way for statues of William Pitt the Elder and the Younger, who epitomize Beckford's political opposite in their loyalty to the king.

49. See the study by Bentham expert Christian Laval, *L'homme économique: Essai sur les racines du néolibéralisme* (Paris: Gallimard, 2007).

50. Bentham again echoes Rousseau's ideas on education.

51. With regard to the modern-day debate, see Shane Bryans, *Prison Governors: Managing Prisons in a Time of Change* (Cullompton: Devon Willan, 2007), in particular 14ff.

52. Jeremy Bentham, *Panopticon*, "Postscript II: A Plan of Management, Part II, Management—in What Hands, and on What Terms" (London, 1791), 19–21.

53. Jeremy Bentham, *Panopticon*, "Postscript II: A Plan of Management, Part VI, Provision for Liberated Prisoners: A Detailed Study of the Appropriateness of Punishments," 224;

Tony Draper, "An Introduction to Jeremy Bentham's Theory of Punishment," *Journal of Bentham Studies* (2002). In 1792, Bentham also drafted guidelines for the management of a Panopticon, entitled "Outline of a Plan for the Management of a Panopticon-Penitentiary House," in *The Works of Jeremy Bentham*, vol. 11, 99–100. See also Bentham's 1830 piece, "The Rationale of Punishment," https://archive.org/details/therationaleofpu00bentuoft.

54. Jeremy Bentham, *Panopticon*, "Postscript II: A Plan of Management, Part II, Management—in What Hands and on What Terms," 54–55.

55. Robert Rolle, *Homo oeconomicus: Wirtschaftsanthropologie in philosophischer Perspektive* (Würzburg: Königshausen u. Neumann, 2005), 117. In this piece, the author posits that Bentham freed "ethics from its subjugation to all religious and metaphysical conditions," basing it instead on entirely scientific premises.

56. See Richard Wrigley and Matthew Craske, eds., *Pantheons: Transformations of a Monumental Idea* (Aldershot: Ashgate, 2004). Bentham mentions the Pantheon in the *Panopticon*, "Postscript 1, Plan of Construction, Part VIII, Inspection Galleries and Lodge," 74.

57. In a footnote at the opening of Paragraph VII—"Chapel"—and Paragraph VIII—"Inspection-Gallery"—in the second postscript of the *Panopticon*, Bentham thanks Reveley at length for his personal contributions to planning the inspection house.

58. In John Bunyan, *The Pilgrim's Progress*, part 1, chapter 3, the author writes:

> When he was got now hard by the hill, it seemed so high, and also that side of it that was next the way-side did hang so much over, that Christian was afraid to venture further, lest the hill should fall on his head; wherefore there he stood still, and wotted not what to do. Also his burden now seemed heavier to him than while he was in his way. There

came also flashes of fire [Ex. 19:16, 18], out of the hill, that made Christian afraid that he should be burnt: here therefore he did sweat and quake for fear [Heb. 12:21]. And now he began to be sorry that he had taken Mr. Worldly Wiseman's counsel; and with that he saw Evangelist coming to meet him, at the sight also of whom he began to blush for shame. So Evangelist drew nearer and nearer; and coming up to him, he looked upon him, with a severe and dreadful countenance, and thus began to reason with Christian.

For more on Bunyan, see Anne Dunan-Page, ed., *The Cambridge Companion to Bunyan* (Cambridge: Cambridge University Press, 2010).

59. Jeremy Bentham, *Panopticon*, "Postscript II. A Plan of Management, Part XI, Schooling and Sunday Employment," 186. For more on Bentham as a critic of the church, see Delos Banning McKown, *Behold the Antichrist: Bentham on Religion* (Amherst: Prometheus Books, 2004). See also James E. Crimmins, ed., *Utilitarians and Religion* (Bristol: Thoemmes, 1998).

60. Bentham connects verses 2, 10, and 9: "2. Thou art about my path, and about my bed: and spiest out all my ways. 10. If I say, Peradventure the darkness shall cover me: then shall my night be turned to day. 9. Even there also shall thy hand lead me: and thy right hand shall hold me." The psalm closes with: "23. Try me, O God, and seek the ground of my heart: prove me, and examine my thoughts. 24. Look well if there be any way of wickedness in me: and lead me in the way everlasting."

61. Georg Stuhlfauth, *Das Dreieck: Die Geschichte eines religiösen Symbols* (Stuttgart: Kohlhammer, 1937).

62. See the works of Lucien Braun, *Bilder der Philosophie* (Darmstadt: Wissenschaftliche Buchgesellschaft, 2010), especially 78ff., 96ff., 109–117ff; and Ralph Konersmann, ed., *Wörterbuch der philosophischen Metaphern* (Darmstadt: Wissenschaftliche Buchgesellschaft, 2007) (entries include "Building,

to build," "Body, Organism," "Light," "Machine," "Room," "Theater"). See also Horst Bredekamp, *Thomas Hobbes visuelle Strategien: Der Leviathan: das Urbild des modernen Staates*, 2nd ed. (Berlin: Akademie, 2001).

63. Christoph Geissmar, *Das Auge Gottes: Bilder zu Jakob Böhme* (Wiesbaden: Harrassowitz, 1993). A relevant text on the symbol's transfer into the secular context is Michael Stolleis, *Das Auge des Gesetzes: Geschichte einer Metapher* (Munich: C. H. Beck, 2004). Its usage traces the spread of the symbol in the Anglican sphere as well, whose theological interpretations of the Trinity varied from the Roman Catholic or Protestant exegeses common in Europe. For a comprehensive introduction, see Gisbert Greshake, *Der dreieine Gott: Eine trinitarische Theologie* (Freiburg: Herder, 2007). See also the widely read contemporary comparative collection: William Jones and Samuel Clarke, *The Catholic Doctrine of a Trinity Proved by Arguments, Expressed in the Terms of the Holy Scripture, with a Few Reflections upon Some Arian Writers* (Oxford, 1756). Furthermore, significant differences existed between conceptions of the divine right of kings in England and France, which also influenced the symbolism of the respective states. In this sense, the argumentation above summarily coarsens things. For example: Ernst Hinrichs, *Fürsten und Mächte: Zum Problem des europäischen Absolutismus* (Göttingen: Vandenhoeck und Ruprecht Verlag, 2000). Regarding the situation in England, see the collection: David Wootton, ed., *Divine Right and Democracy: An Anthology of Political Writing in Stuart England* (Harmondsworth: Penguin Books, 1986).

64. Milne, *The Correspondence of Jeremy Bentham*, Letter 735, Reveley to Bentham, January 11, 1791. The following quotation: ibid., Bentham to John Parnell, February 1, 1791, Letter 741, p. 232.

65. For more on Enlightenment conceptions of God, see John Gascoigne, *Science, Philosophy and Religion in the Age of Enlightenment: British and Global Contexts* (Farnham: Routledge,

2010). On reactions to Newton, see Fritz Wagner, *Zur Apotheose Newtons: Künstlerische Utopie und naturwissenschaftliches Weltbild* (Munich: Verlag der Bayerischen Akademie der Wissenschaften, 1974). See also Stuart Peterfreund, *William Blake in a Newtonian World: Essays on Literature as Art and Science* (Norman: University of Oklahoma Press, 1998); Mordechai Feingold, *The Newtonian Moment: Isaac Newton and the Making of Modern Culture* (Oxford: Oxford University Press, 2004); László Földényi, *Newtons Traum: Blakes Newton* (Berlin: Matthes & Seitz, 2005); Milo Keynes, *The Iconography of Sir Isaac Newton to 1800* (Woodbridge: Boydell Press, 2005); Michael Neumann and Andreas Hartmann, eds., *Mythen Europas: Schlüsselfiguren der Imagination*, vol. 5, *Vom Barock zur Aufklärung* (Regensburg: F. Pustet, 2007); Heinz Herbert Mann, *Augenglas und Perspektiv: Studien zur Ikonographie zweier Bildmotive* (Berlin: Gebr. Mann, 1992). For more on the medieval representation of astronomy, see Kathrin Müller, *Visuelle Weltaneignung: Astronomische und kosmologische Diagramme in Handschriften des Mittelalters* (Göttingen: Vandenhoeck & Ruprecht, 2008).

66. Thomas Smith Webb, *The Freemason's Monitor, or Illustrations of Masonry*, 2nd ed. (Salem: Cushing and Appleton, 1818), 35. According to a February 22, 2011, conversation with Philip Schofield, Bentham was a Freemason. The claim could not be substantiated in the archives at Freemasons' Hall in London. Proof could not be found for Reveley's membership, either. For more on symbolism, see Victoria Salt Dennis, *Discovering Friendly and Fraternal Societies: Their Badges and Regalia* (Princes Risborough: Shire Publications, 2005). See also Anthony Gerbino and Stephen Johnston, eds., *Compass and Rule: Architecture as Mathematical Practice in England 1500–1750* (New Haven, CT: Yale University Press, 2009). In his painting, *A Philosopher Lecturing on the Orrery* (1766, Derby Museum), the painter Joseph Wright of Derby depicts the abduction of science and technology by the humanities. See Paul Duro, "'Great and Noble Ideas of the

Moral Kind': Wright of Derby and the Scientific Sublime," in *Art History* 33, no. 4 (2010): 660–679. See also Sabine Krifka, *Wright of Derby: Schauplätze der Wissenschaft* (Aachen: Mainz, 1996). Johannes Kepler's *Harmonices Mundi* serves as an antecedent: "God, like a human architect, approached the founding of the world according to order and rule and measured everything in such a manner, that one might think not art took nature for an example but God Himself, in the course of His creation took the art of man as an example." Quoted from the 1939 German edition (Reprint Munich, 2006), 15.

67. It is tempting to claim a connection between the ground plan of the Panopticon and the discoidal depictions of cosmic and political systems popularized in the Middle Ages; however, such a connection is impossible to prove, based on Bentham's own statements. See Karl Clausberg, *Kosmische Visionen: Mystische Weltbilder von Hildegard von Bingen bis heute* (Cologne: DuMont Reiseverlag, 1980). On the reciprocity between state utopia and science in England, see Paul A. Olson, *The Kingdom of Science: Literary Utopianism and British Education 1612–1870* (Lincoln: University of Nebraska Press, 2002). Bentham himself revisits this claim in his reflections, where he writes that the Panopticon was "a magnificent instrument with which I then dreamed of revolutionizing the world." See *The Works of Jeremy Bentham*, vol. 10, 572.

68. Jeremy Bentham, *Panopticon*, "Postscript I: Plan of Construction, Part VIII, Inspection-Galleries and Lodge," 75.

69. John Dewey, "Intelligence of Morals," in *The Influence of Darwin on Philosophy and Other Essays* (New York: Henry Holt, 1910), 61–62. Dewey continues: "The notion that laws govern and forces rule is an animistic survival. It is a product of reading nature in terms of politics in order to turn around and then read politics in the light of supposed sanctions of nature. This idea passed from medieval theology into the science of Newton, to whom the universe was the dominion of a sovereign whose laws were the laws of nature. From Newton it passed

into the deism of the eighteenth century, whence it migrated into the philosophy of the Enlightenment, to make its last stand in Spencer's philosophy of the fixed environment and the static goal."

70. See Thomas Philip Schofield, "Jeremy Bentham und die englische Jurisprudenz im 19. Jahrhundert," in *Der klassische Utilitarismus: Einflüsse, Entwicklungen, Folgen*, ed. Ulrich Gähde and Wolfgang Schrader (Berlin: Akademie, 1992), 35.

71. Jeremy Bentham, *Introduction to the Principles of Morals and Legislation* (London, 1789), chap. 1, "The Principle of Utility." Republished as *The Collected Works of Jeremy Bentham*, vol. 1. See Jon Parkin, *Science, Religion and Politics in Restoration England: Richard Cumberland's De Legibus Naturae* (Woodbridge: Royal Historical Society, 1999).

72. Original formulation in Günter Hartfiel, Wirtschaftliche und soziale Rationalität (Stuttgart: Enke, 1968), 97, quoted here from Robert Rolle, *Homo oeconomicus: Wirtschaftsanthropologie in philosophischer Perspektive* (Würzburg: Königshausen u. Neumann, 2005), 116. Regarding the following, see Bentham's essay, "The Influence of Time and Place on Legislation," in *The Works of Jeremy Bentham*, vol. 1, 171ff.

73. Bentham's "felicific calculus," discussed in chapters 4 ("Value of a Lot of Pleasure or Pain, How to be Measured") and 5 ("Pleasures and Pains, their Kinds") of the *Introduction to the Principles of Moral and Legislation*, is discussed in every introduction to Bentham and utilitarianism. The full text is available online. More recent pieces on the topic include Antoinette Baujard, "From Moral Welfarism to Technical Non-Welfarism: A Step Back to Bentham's Felicific Calculus," *European Journal of the History of Economic Thought* 16, no. 3 (Sept. 2009): 431–453, and Antoinette Baujard, "Collective Interest vs. Individual Interest in Bentham's Felicific Calculus: Questioning Welfarism and Fairness," *European Journal of the History of Economic Thought* 17, no. 4 (Oct. 2010):

607–634. The idea of morality as experimental science can also be found in David Hume's writings.

74. Jeremy Bentham, *Introduction to the Principles of Morals and Legislation*, chap. 4.

75. Johann Wolfgang Goethe, *Maximen und Reflexionen, Über Literatur und Ethik, III*, 160 (Frankfurt, 1989), sec. 1, vol. 10, 767: "Das Gesicht ist der edelste Sinn; die andern vier belehren uns nur durch die Organe des Takts: Wir hören, wir fühlen, riechen und betasten alles durch Berührung; das Gesicht aber steht unendlich höher, verfeint sich über die Materie und nähert sich den Fähigkeiten des Geistes [The face is the noblest sense; the other four only instruct us through the tactile organs: we hear, we sense, smell, and feel everything through touch; but the face resides infinitely higher, cultivates itself beyond matter, and approaches the capabilities of the mind]." The stratification of the senses was reliably contentious. Within his hierarchy of the senses, Immanuel Kant deemed vision the most important, an opinion not universally shared over the course of the eighteenth century. For an extensive survey of the topic, see Alexandra Hildebrandt, *"Lebwohl, du heitrer Schein!" Blindheit im Kontext der Romantik* (Würzburg: Königshausen & Neumann, 2002), 24, n. 1. See also Kant's original text, "Anthropologie in pragmatischer Hinsicht" (1798), https://archive.org/details/immanuelkant san00kantgoog. The cultural historical "expansion" of eyesight, prompted in part by Newton's telescope, can also be traced back to Johannes Kepler and René Descartes's "dioptric" antecedents. Essential reading on eyesight, optics, and mathematics is Robert Smith, *A Compleat System of Opticks* (Cambridge, 1738). In this context, see also Henry Steffens, *The Development of Newtonian Optics in England* (New York: Watson, 1977). See also the entry "Sehe-Kunst" in J. H. Zedler's *Grosses Universal-Lexicon* (Leipzig, 1732–1750), vol. 36, 668ff.

76. The etymology of the term traces its usage for optical devices/ telescopes to the mid-eighteenth century. Bentham employs the unifying syllable "pan" in other writings as an expression of universality in his proposed concepts. He referred to his "Constitutional Code" as "my all-comprehensive Code (or say, in one word, of my Pannomion)." *The Works of Jeremy Bentham*, vol. 19, 146 (Constitutional Code, Book 2, preface). For more on reciprocity between the disciplines with regard to the metaphor of light, see Richard Panek, *Das Auge Gottes: Das Teleskop und die lange Entdeckung der Unendlichkeit* (Stuttgart: Klett-Cotta Verlag, 2001); Jean-Pierre Changeux, ed., *La lumière au siècle des Lumières et aujourd'hui* (Paris: Odile Jacob, 2005), esp. the essays on 52–67 and 136–143. See also Linda Báez-Rubí, "'Et remotissima propre': Das Fernrohr als Gerät des Sehens und Träger der Vision im 17. und 18. Jahrhundert," in *Techniken des Bildes*, Martin Schulz and Beat Wyss (Munich: Fink, 2010).

77. Stephan Oettermann, *Das Panorama: Die Geschichte eines Massenmediums* (Frankfurt: Syndikat, 1980). Of the extensive literature on the topic, see also pieces published by the International Panorama Council. On the rise of consumer culture generally, see John Brewer und Roy Porter, *Consumption and the World of Goods* (London: Routledge, 1993).

78. *The Works of Jeremy Bentham*, vol. 11, 107. On music in the Panopticon, see Semple, *Bentham's Prison*, 284.

79. Jeremy Bentham, *Panopticon*, "Postscript I: Plan of Construction,Part VII, Chapel," 57: "A mask affords it at once. Guilt will thus be pilloried in the abstract." For a detailed examination of the Panopticon as theater, see Miran Božovič, "An Utterly Dark Spot," in Jeremy Bentham, *The Panopticon Writings* (London: Verso, 1995), 1–27. See also (in German, including an essay on the Auto-Icon) Miran Božovič, *... Was Du nicht siehst: Blick und Körper 1700/1800* (Zurich: Diaphanes, 2006), 103ff. For a similarly sweeping view on Bentham, see David Collings, *Monstrous Society: Reciprocity, Discipline, and the*

Political Uncanny, c. 1780–1848 (Lewisburg, PA: Bucknell University Press, 2009), esp. 95–130.

80. Until 1770, Bedlam (Bethlehem Hospital) was open to the paying public. Jonathan Andrews, *Bedlam Revisited: A History of Bethlem Hospital* (London: University of London, 1991). See also Patricia Allderidge, *Bethlem Hospital 1247–1997: A Pictorial Record* (Chichester: Phillimore, 1997). For further context, see Roy Porter, *Madmen: A Social History of Mad-houses, Mad-doctors and Lunatics* (Stroud: Tempus, 2006).

81. See the essays in Wolfgang Cilleßen and Rolf Reichardt, eds., *Revolution und Gegenrevolution in der europäischen Bildpublizistik 1789–1889* (Hildesheim: Olms, 2010).

82. In the mid-nineteenth century, the meaning of "panorama" shifted to crude fairground spectacles, such as freak shows and curiosity cabinets—a shift from "showing" to "exposing."

83. Jeremy Bentham, *Panopticon*, "Postscript II: A Plan of Management, Part II," 53. Symbolic punishment displays striking parallels to Masonic traditions, which repeatedly surface in Bentham's works. See the entry "Punishment" in the *Encyclopaedia of Freemasonry*, vol. 2 (London, 1909), 759–760. Bentham's ties to freemasonry have not been researched.

84. Undated letter from Bentham (Nov. 1791) to the French National Assembly (Jean-Philippe Garran-Coulon). In Basil Montagu, ed., *The Opinions of Different Authors upon the Punishment of Death*, vol. 1 (London: Longman, Hurst, Rees, Orme and Brown, 1813), 322–323. See also further letters, *The Works of Jeremy Bentham*, vol. 10, 269ff. Plans for his own home—which was to feature Panopticon memorabilia and allusions (including a circular fishbowl)—underscore Bentham's earnestness. Further details in Semple, *Bentham's Prison*, 296.

THE AUTO-ICON

1. The 1769 document is cited in John Timbs, *English Eccentrics and Eccentricities* (London: Richard Bentley, 1866), 180.

2.   Jeremy Bentham, "Constitutional Code," book 2, preface, in *The Works of Jeremy Bentham* (Edinburgh: John Bowring, 1838–1843), vol. 9, 146.

3.   At present, only rudimentary research has been done on Bentham's impact on international politics. Existing studies include Jürgen Samtleben, "Menschheitsglück und Gesetzgebungsexport: Zu Jeremy Benthams Wirkung in Lateinamerika," in *Rechtspraxis und Rechtskultur in Brasilien und Lateinamerika: Beiträge aus internationaler und regionaler Perspektive* (Aachen: Shaker, 2010), 231–343. The term "legislator of the world" is attributed to the Guatemalan politician José del Valle. See Philip Schofield, "Jeremy Bentham: Legislator of the World," in *Legal Theory at the End of the Millennium*, ed. Michael D. A. Freeman (Oxford: Oxford University Press, 1998), 115–148.

4.   University College London, Special Collections Department, Bentham Collection 9/123, Codicil from March 29/October 9, 1824 (copy).

5.   See "Auto-Ikone oder utilitaristische Meditationen über den eigenen Körper," in Miran Božovič, ... *Was Du nicht siehst: Blick und Körper 1700, 1800* (Zurich: Diaphanes, 2006), 125–144.

6.   Jeremy Bentham, "Auto-Icon, or Farther Uses of the Dead to the Living, in *Jeremy Bentham's Auto-Icon and Related Writings*, James Crimmins (London: Thoemmes Continuum, 2002).

7.   As seen in Charles Millard's obituary, a "demonstrator" and lecturer at the Webb Street School of Anatomy, who died at age twenty-seven. "Obituaries," *Gentleman's Magazine* 5 (June 1836): 671.

8.   Text cited in Ruth Richardson and Brian Hurwitz, "Jeremy Bentham's Self Image: An Exemplary Bequest for Dissection," *British Medical Journal* 295 (July 18, 1987): 195. The following quotation ("If the dead bodies ...") is also drawn from this text. See also Ruth Richardson, "Bentham and Bodies for Dissection," *Bentham Newsletter* 10 (1986): 22–33.

9. Beside the extensive literature on Burke and Hare (including Stevenson's tale of the "body snatchers" and film versions, such as Boris Karloff's 1945 *The Body Snatcher*), important pieces on the subject include Ruth Richardson, *Death, Dissection and the Destitute* (London: Routledge & Kegan Paul, 1987; new ed. Chicago: University of Chicago Press, 2000). See also Wendy Moore, *The Knife Man: Blood, Body-Snatching and the Birth of Surgery* (London: Broadway Books, 2005). See also Claudia Benthien and Christoph Wulf, eds., *Körperteile: Eine kulturelle Anatomie* (Reinbek: Rowohlt Taschenbuch, 2001). On representations of surgery in art, see Fiona Haslam, *From Hogarth to Rowlandson: Medicine in Art in Eighteenth-Century Britain* (Liverpool: Liverpool University Press, 1996). On mesmerism, see Ernst Florey, *Ars magnetica: Franz Anton Mesmer (1734–1815) Magier vom Bodensee* (Konstanz: Universitätsverlag Konstanz, 1995).

10. See Ruth Richardson and Brian Hurwitz, "Jeremy Bentham's Self Image: An Exemplary Bequest for Dissection," *British Medical Journal* 295 (July 18, 1987): 197, which also includes information on the bill and its contents. See also Ian R. Burney, *Bodies of Evidence: Medicine and the Politics of the English Inquest, 1830–1926* (Baltimore: Johns Hopkins University Press, 2000).

11. June 8 was a Friday. Several sources and studies also cite the ninth as the date of the lecture.

12. W. J. Fox's report (continued after the next paragraph) was first published in the *Monthly Repository* 67, n.s. (July 1832): 450; selection here drawn from John Timbs, *English Eccentrics and Eccentricities*, 180–181. Robert Bentley Todd documented many London vivisections in *Cyclopaedia of Anatomy and Physiology* (London: Sherwood, Gilbert, and Piper, 1836).

13. See the invitation to "Dr. Armstrong's Lecture on the Morbid Anatomy, Nature and Treatment of Acute and Chronic Diseases," *London Literary Gazette and Journal of Belles Lettres, Arts, Sciences, etc.* 593 (May 31, 1828): 350. This may be the

very Dr. Armstrong named in Bentham's 1824 will, before being replaced by Southwood Smith as the heir to Bentham's body.

14. See Andrew Cunningham and Roger Kenneth French, *The Medical Enlightenment of the Eighteenth-Century* (Cambridge: Cambridge University Press, 1990), esp. Adrian Wilson's essay. On aspects of the conflict between medicine and the Church, see Andrew Cunningham and Ole Peter Grell, eds., *Medicine and Religion in Enlightenment Europe* (Aldershot: Ashgate, 2007). There are only a few scattered references online to the Webb Street School of Anatomy, which apparently closed in the mid-nineteenth century.

15. William Munk, *The Roll of the Royal College of Physicians of London*, 2nd ed., 3 vols. (London, 1878), vol. 2, 237. The quotation can also be found in "Southwood Smith," in the *Dictionary of National Biography*, as well as in C. F. A. Marmoy's essay, "The 'Auto-Icon' of Jeremy Bentham at University College, London," *Medical History* 2, no. 2 (April 1958).

16. Quoted from Martin Luther's translation (Stuttgart: Deutsche Bibelgesellschaft, 1985).

17. Jeremy Bentham, diary entry, May 4, 1822, quoted in Stephen Conway, "Bentham on Peace and War," *Utilitas* 1 (1989): 93, n. 73.

18. Excerpts of Southwood Smith's speech were first printed in *Monthly Repository* 67, n.s. (July 1832): 450–458 ("On the Character and Philosophy of the Late Jeremy Bentham"); this quotation can be found on 451. On Bentham's criticism of religion, see James E. Crimmins, *Secular Utilitarianism: Social Science and the Critique of Religion in the Thought of Jeremy Bentham* (Oxford: Clarendon Press, 1990). See also McKown, *Behold the Antichrist: Bentham on Religion* (Amherst: Prometheus Books, 2004)

19. On *mokomokai* and their reception, see Horatio Gordon Robley, *Moko, or Maori Tattooing* (London: Chapman and Hall,

1896). See also Amiria Henare, *Museums, Anthropology and Material Exchange* (Cambridge: Cambridge University Press, 2005); Elizabeth Edwards, Chris Gosden, and Ruth B. Phillips, eds., *Sensible Objects: Colonialism, Museums and Material Culture* (Oxford: Berg, 2006); Conal McCarthy, *Exhibiting Maori: A History of Colonial Cultures of Display* (Oxford: Berg, 2007). Māori culture has received renewed attention in recent years, thanks in part to New Zealand's demands for restitutions from institutions like the British Museum.

20. The will is quoted here: University College London, Special Collections Department, Bentham Collection 9/123, Codicil from March 29/October 9, 1824 (copy). A fragment dated June 26, 1820 (with post hoc annotation) from Bentham to Edwin Chadwick uses the term "Auto-Icon," possibly for the first time: University College London, Special Collections Department, Bentham Collection, 149/203.

21. Bentham, *Auto-Icon, or Farther Uses of the Dead to the Living*.

22. For a detailed account of the experiments, see James E. Crimmins, "Introduction," in *Jeremy Bentham's Auto-Icon and Related Writings* (Bristol: Thoemmes Continuum, 2002). See also C. F. A. Marmoy, "The 'Auto-Icon' of Jeremy Bentham at University College London," *Medical History* 2 (1958): 77–86. Marmoy also discusses various legends and their backgrounds. In Bentham's manuscript, "Auto-Icon," on the possibility of discoloration during the dehydration process, he writes: "In colour only is there any considerable change; and colour may be easily supplied." A further aspect worth noting is the question as to whether the "Auto-Icon" manuscript is a forgery, as argued in the late nineteenth century (and hoped for by many Bentham enthusiasts).

23. Since C. F. A. Marmoy's "The 'Auto-Icon' of Jeremy Bentham," it is commonly accepted that Talrich created the Auto-Icon's head. For more on Talrich generally, see Michel Lemire,

Artistes et mortels (Paris: Raymond Chabaud, 1990), 345–363.

24. Bentham's acquaintance Henry Brougham, as cited in Catherine Fuller, *The Old Radical: Representations of Jeremy Bentham* (London: UCL Art Collections, 1998), 5. This brief catalog is fundamental in understanding visual depictions of Bentham, including details on d'Angers, 39–41, or the Auto-Icon, 9–14, 50–53. See also Southwood Smith's letter to John Bowring on March 3, 1833, regarding the Auto-Icon's hair: University College London, Special Collections Department, Bentham Collection 173/32a; and Southwood Smith's remarks on the similarity between the Auto-Icon and Bentham, quoted in Marmoy, "The 'Auto-Icon' of Jeremy Bentham," 82. It is uncertain whether a death mask was made for Bentham. A mask in the collection at the Edinburgh Phrenological Society—possibly another model for the wax head—was most likely created during Bentham's lifetime. See *Phrenological Journal and Magazine of Moral Science* (1838). See also Rüdiger Campe and Manfred Schneider, eds., *Geschichten der Physiognomik: Text, Bild, Wissen* (Freiburg: Rombach, 1994); Bernhard Maaz, *Vom Kult des Genies: David d'Angers' Bildnisse von Goethe bis Caspar David Friedrich* (Munich: Deutscher Kunstverlag, 2004).

25. "Annual Biography and Obituary, 1833," 363, quoted in the *Dictionary of National Biography: From the Earliest Times to 1900* (London: Oxford University Press, 1949).

26. University College London, Special Collections Department, Bentham Collection 9/123, Codicil from March 29/October 9, 1824 (copy). See also Bentham's final will (1832), cited in Marmoy, "The 'Auto-Icon' of Jeremy Bentham," 80; and Bentham, *Auto-Icon, or Farther Uses of the Dead to the Living*: "But when Bentham has ceased to live, (in memory will he never cease to live!) whom shall the Bentham-Club have for its chairman? Whom but Bentham itself? On him will all eyes be turned,—to him all speeches be addressed."

27. According to a conversation with Philip Schofield, director of the Bentham Project at University College London, on February 22, 2011. See also Jan Gerchow, ed., *Ebenbilder: Kopien von Körpern: Modelle des Menschen* (Ostfildern-Ruit: Hatje Cantz, 2002). This catalog corresponds to an exhibit the Auto-Icon "visited" in Essen, after having been to the city once already, as part of the 1992 show, Metropole London.

28. The classic text on this topic is Edith Sitwell, *English Eccentrics* (London: Faber & Faber, 1933). See also Catherine Caufield, *The Man Who Ate Bluebottles: And Other Great British Eccentrics* (Thriplow: Totem Books, 2005); Henry Hemming, *In Search of the English Eccentric* (London: John Murray, 2009); Jules Barbey d'Aurevilly, *Du Dandysme et de George Brummell* (Caen: B. Mancel, 1845). For more on Bentham as an eccentric, see Timbs, *English Eccentrics and Eccentricities*, 179–180, who enumerates other stipulations in the will, from 172.

29. Timbs, *English Eccentrics and Eccentricities*, 177.

30. Algernon Charles Swinburne, *William Blake: A Critical Essay* (London: J. C. Hotten, 1868), 1.

31. Exemplary in a crowded field is Helmar Schramm and Ludger Schwarte, eds., *Kunstkammer, Laboratorium, Bühne: Schauplätze des Wissens im 17: Jahrhundert* (Berlin: De Gruyter, 2003). See also Susanne König-Lein, ed., *Weltenharmonie: Die Kunstkammer und die Ordnung des Wissens* (Braunschweig: Herzog Anton Ulrich-Museum Braunschweig, 2000); Horst Bredekamp, *Antikensehnsucht und Maschinenglaube: Die Geschichte der Kunstkammer und die Zukunft der Kunstgeschichte*, new ed. (Berlin: Wagenbach, 2000).

32. On the connections between science, perception, art, and their representation around 1800, see Gabriele Dürbeck and Bettina Gockel, eds., *Wahrnehmung der Natur, Natur der Wahrnehmung: Studien zur Geschichte visueller Kultur um 1800* (Dresden: Verlag der Kunst, 2001).

33. Anthony Harvey and Richard Mortimer, eds., *Funeral Effigies of Westminster Abbey* (Woodbridge: Boydell Press, 2003). For a general study, among many, see Julius von Schlosser, *Tote Blicke: Geschichte der Portraitbildnerei in Wachs, Ein Versuch* (1911), ed. Thomas Medicus (Berlin: Akademie, 1993). See also Adolf Reinle, *Das stellvertretende Bildnis* (Zurich: Artemis, 1984); Susann Waldmann, *Die lebensgroße Wachsfigur: Eine Studie zu Funktion und Bedeutung der keroplastischen Portraitfigur vom Spätmittelalter bis zum 18, Jahrhundert* (Munich, 1990); Nigel Llewellyn, *The Art of Death 1500–1800* (London: Reaktion Books, 1991); Andrea Klier, *Fixierte Natur: Naturabguß und Effigies im 16. Jahrhundert* (Berlin: Reimer, 2003); Sergio Bertelli, *The King's Body: The Sacred Rituals of Power in Medieval and Early Modern Europe* (University Park: Penn State University Press, 2001); Hasso Hofmann, *Repräsentation: Studien zur Wort- und Begriffsgeschichte von der Antike bis ins 19. Jahrhundert*, 4th ed. (Berlin: Duncker & Humblot, 2003). For more on effigies in France, see Daniel Payot, *Effigies: La notion d'art et les fins de la ressemblance* (Paris: Galilée, 1997). See also the catalog *Royales effigies* (Chambéry, 1985). Information on effigies in Bentham's time is compiled in encyclopedias by Diderot, Zedler, and Krünitz, as well as the *Encyclopedia Britannica*.

34. See Ernst Kantorowicz, *The King's Two Bodies: A Study in Medieval Political Theology* (Princeton, NJ: Princeton University Press, 1957).

35. The seminal work on this is Pamela Pilbeam, *Madame Tussaud and the History of Waxworks* (London: Bloomsbury Academic, 2003). See also Uta Kornmeier, "Taken from Life: Madame Tussaud und die Geschichte des Wachsfigurenkabinetts vom 17. bis frühen 20, Jahrhundert," PhD dissertation, Humboldt University, Berlin, 2006. Ron Mueck, Duane Hanson, and other artists' works demonstrate the ongoing interest in waxworks today.

36. For more on Rastatt, see Sigrid Gensichen, *Schloss Favorite Rastatt mit Garten und Eremitage* (Munich: Deutscher Kunstverlag, 2007). For more on dinners with Curtius in Paris, see Pilbeam, *Madame Tussaud and the History of Waxworks*, 27–30.

37. Harvey and Mortimer, eds., *The Funeral Effigies of Westminster Abbey*, 181. For more on the "ragged regiment" and the boys of Westminster School, see Pilbeam, *Madame Tussaud and the History of Waxworks*, 2.

38. Bentham, *Auto-Icon, or Farther Uses of the Dead to the Living*. See also David Bindman, "The Skeleton in the Cupboard: Jeremy Bentham's Auto-Icon," in Catherine Fuller, *The Old Radical: Representations of Bentham* (London: UCL Art Collections, 1998), 9. Bindman cites Andrew Hemingway, "Genius, Gender and Progress: Benthamism and the Arts in the 1820s," *Art History* 16 (1993): 621.

39. Ranelagh was one of many strolling grounds in London equipped with a circular central structure for indoor walking; a central shaft within the structure boasted built-in tearooms, and the outside was flanked with galleries that allowed viewers to watch the flâneurs. The ground plan and basic idea can certainly be seen as antecedents to the Panopticon. Karl Philipp Moritz wrote about Ranelagh after visiting on a 1782 trip to England. See also Terry Castle, *Masquerade and Civilization: The Carnivalesque in Eighteenth-Century English Culture and Fiction* (Stanford: Stanford University Press, 1986). Alongside these descriptions of London, Sébastien Mercier's "Tableau de Paris" (1782–1788), https://archive.org/details/tableaudeparis01mergoog, and the *Cent-et-un* books (15 vols., 1831–1834) provide a comprehensive look at French popular culture.

40. Alexander Meyrick Broadley compiles the massive number of Napoleon caricatures in *Napoleon in Caricature 1795–1821*, 2 vols. (London: John Lane, 1911). For more on the many facets of Napoleonic visual propaganda, see George Vilinbachov and

Magnus Olausson, eds., *Staging Power: Napoleon, Charles John, Alexander* (Stockholm: Nationalmuseum/The State Hermitage Museum, 2010). See also Dimitri Casali and David Chanteranne, *Napoléon par les peintres* (Paris: Editions du Seuil, 2009).

41. Pilbeam, *Madame Tussaud and the History of Waxworks*, 7. On Madame Tussaud's philosophers and their predecessors, see Kornmeier, "Taken from Life," 47, 52, 65, 137, 158, 222, 227.

42. Fyodor Dostoevsky describes the painting's effect in *The Idiot*, part 2, chap. 4: "'Why, some people's faith is ruined by that picture!'" See Kristin Marek, *Der Leichnam als Bild, der Leichnam im Bild*. For more on the *Body of the Dead Christ in the Tomb*, by Hans Holbein the Younger, and its modern derivatives, see *Die neue Sichtbarkeit des Todes*, ed. Thomas Macho and Kristin Marek (Munich: Fink, 2007), 295–313. See also Mark Roskill and John Oliver Hand, *Hans Holbein: Paintings, Prints and Reception* (New Haven: Yale University Press, 2001), 83–95, 187–209. For an important collection of sources, see Ludwig Choulant, *Geschichte und Bibliographie der anatomischen Abbildung nach ihrer Beziehung auf anatomische Wissenschaft und bildende Kunst, nebst einer Auswahl von Illustrationen nach berühmten Künstlern, Hans Holbein, Lionardo da Vinci, Rafael* (Leipzig: R. Weigel, 1852; reprint Wiesbaden: Niederwalluf Sändig, 1971). For information on the phenomenon more generally, see Morwena Joly, *La leçon d'anatomie: Le corps des artistes de la Renaissance au romantisme* (Paris: Hazan, 2008). See also Philippe Comar, ed., *Figures du corps: Une leçon d'anatomie à l'École des Beaux-Arts* (Paris: ENSBA, 2008).

43. Jörg Trempler, "Der Stil des Augenblicks: Das Bild zum Bericht," in Jean Baptiste Savigny and Alexandre Corréard, *Der Schiffbruch der Fregatte Medusa* (Berlin: Matthes & Seitz, 2005), 191–240. In 1820, forty thousand visitors poured in to view Géricault's work, exhibited in London's temple of entertainment, the so-called Egyptian Halls. See Patrick Noon and

Stephen Bann, *Crossing the Channel: British and French Painting in the Age of Romanticism* (London: Tate Publishing, 2003). For context, see Darcy Grimaldo Grigsby, *Extremities: Painting Empire in Post-Revolutionary France* (New Haven, CT: Yale University Press, 2002). For more on Rembrandt, see Claus Volkenandt, *Rembrandt: Anatomie eines Bildes* (Munich: Fink, 2004).

44. Evelyne Barbin and Dominique Le Nen, eds., *Sciences et arts: Représentations du corps et matériaux de l'art* (Paris: Vuibert, 2009), esp. Bruno Lussiez, "Anatomie de la crucifixion," 47–65.

45. Felice Fontana, a Florentine doctor and wax sculptor was the owner of this collection at the Josephinum Medical Museum in Vienna; see Manfred Skopec, ed., *Anatomie als Kunst: Anatomische Wachsmodelle des 18. Jahrhunderts im Josephinum in Wien* (Vienna: Brandstätter, 2002). For more on the pregnant figures in London, see Pilbeam, *Madame Tussaud and the History of Waxworks*, 6. Goethe wrote a text on the use of wax figures entitled "Plastic Anatomy" in 1832. See Frank Druffner, "Identität statt Ähnlichkeit: Jeremy Benthams 'Auto-Icon,'" *Zeitschrift für Ideengeschichte* 1, no. 3 (2007): 87.

46. William Hogarth, *The Analysis of Beauty*, new ed. (London, 1772). For more on Hogarth, see David Bindman and Frédéric Ogée, eds., *Hogarth: Representing Nature's Machines* (Manchester: Manchester University Press, 2001). Chapter 9 ("Of Consciousness") in Bentham's *Introduction to the Principles of Morals and Legislation* exemplifies the disinterest in epistemological or metaphysical questioning. Burke's *Philosophical Enquiry into the Origin of Our Ideas of the Sublime and Beautiful* (London, 1757) also attempted to categorize taste scientifically—to objectify the subjective—thus oscillating between scientific claims and epistemological doubt.

47. John Stuart Mill, "Bentham, Section 2: Limits of Bentham's Method," in *Jeremy Bentham: Ten Critical Essays*, ed. Bhikhu C. Parekh (London: Routledge, 1974), 16.

48. Karl Marx and Friedrich Engels, *Collected Works*, vol. 1, sec. 3, letter from November 18, 1844, 251–252.

49. This and the previous quotations from Jeremy Bentham, *Auto-Icon, or, Farther Uses of the Dead to the Living*.

50. Hans-Joachim Störig, *Kleine Weltgeschichte der Philosophie*, rev. ed. (Frankfurt: Fischer, 2003), 431.

PRACTICE AFTER THEORY

1. Karl Marx, *Capital*, vol. 1, in Karl Marx, Friedrich Engels, *Collected Works*, vol. 23 (Berlin, 1970), 189ff and 636ff. See Wilhelm Hofmann, *Politik des aufgeklärten Glücks: Jeremy Benthams philosophisch-politisches Denken* (Berlin: De Gruyter, 2002), 45. In his 1844 book *Utilitarianism Unmasked*, Bentham's former secretary, John Flowerdew Colls—who found religion after the decline of utilitarianism—attempted to discredit the philosophy by describing Bentham's personal idiosyncrasies. See Stephen Conway, "J. F. Colls, M. A. Gathercole, and Utilitarianism Unmasked: A Neglected Episode in the Anglican Response to Bentham," *Journal of Ecclesiastical History* 45 (1994): 435–447.

2. Adam Smith, *The Wealth of Nations: An Inquiry into the Nature and Causes of the Wealth of Nations*, book 4, chap. 2 (London, 1776).

3. The following discussion is supported by Joseph Vogl, *Das Gespenst des Kapitals* (Zurich: Diaphanes, 2010). See also the classic criticism of liberalism/capitalism by Karl Polanyi, *The Great Transformation: Politische und ökonomische Ursprünge von Gesellschaften und Wirtschaftssystemen* (1944; Frankfurt: Suhrkamp, 1990). See also Niall Ferguson, *The Ascent of Money: A Financial History of the World* (London: Penguin, 2009); Peter Sloderdijk, *Im Weltinnenraum des Kapitals: Für eine philosophische Theorie der Globalisierung* (Frankfurt: Suhrkamp, 2005).

4.   For an introduction to charlatanry, see Joachim Kalka, *Phantome der Aufklärung: Von Geistern, Schwindlern und dem Perpetuum mobile* (Berlin: Berenberg, 2006). In *The Ghost-Seer*, Schiller asks, "Would you rather give credit to a miracle than admit an improbability?" and "What do all these wonders prove, if I can demonstrate that a single one among them is a manifest deception?"

5.   Edmund Burke: *A Philosophical Enquiry into the Origin of our Ideas of the Sublime and Beautiful* (1757), part 2, sec. 3 (Oxford: Oxford University Press, 1990), 54.

6.   For more on the development of Panopticon prisons after Bentham, see the afterword to the German edition of Jeremy Bentham's *Panopticon*, ed. Christian Welzbacher (Berlin: Matthes & Seitz, 2011).

7.   See Barbara Dienst, *Der Kosmos des Peter Flötner: Eine Bildwelt der Renaissance in Deutschland* (Munich: Deutscher Kunstverlag, 2002). See also Werner Hofmann, ed., *Luther und die Folgen für die Kunst* (Munich: Prestel, 1983), 186.

8.   Morna O'Neill, *Walter Crane: The Arts and Crafts, Painting, and Politics, 1875–1890* (New Haven, CT: Yale University Press, 2010).

9.   For more on the seemingly implicit connection between "purity" as a virtue of those individuals striving for personal gain and efficiency, see Manuel Frey, *Der reinliche Bürger: Entstehung und Verbreitung bürgerlicher Tugenden in Deutschland 1760–1860* (Göttingen: Vandenhoeck & Ruprecht, 1997).

10.   Massachusetts History Society, http://www.masshist.org/jqadiaries/doc.cfm?id=jqad38_319. See also Marion G. Müller, *Politische Bildstrategien im amerikanischen Präsidentschaftswahlkampf 1828–1996* (Berlin: De Gruyter, 1997).

11.   For more on the characteristic entanglement of state and capital in the United States, see Andrew Ross Sorkin, *Too Big to Fail: The Inside Story of How Wall Street and Washington*

Fought to Save the Financial System—and Themselves (New York: Viking, 2009). See also Simon Johnson and James Kwak, *13 Bankers: The Wall Street Takeover and the Next Financial Meltdown* (New York: Pantheon, 2010).

12. See the "Skyscraper Index," which charts a direct relationship between skyscraper height and the likelihood of economic downturn, in Andrew Lawrence, *The Skyscraper Index: Faulty Towers*, Property Report, created for investment bank Dresdner Kleinwort Wasserstein in January 1999. See also Carol Willis, *Form Follows Finance: Skyscrapers and Skylines of New York and Chicago* (Princeton, NJ: Princeton Architectural Press, 1995).

13. John W. Reps, *Monumental Washington: The Planning and Development of the Capital Center* (Princeton, NJ: Princeton University Press, 1967). See also Wolfgang Sonne, *Representing the State: Capital City Planning in the Early 20th Century* (Berlin: Prestel, 2003).